THE TEENAGE HEALTHYPRENEUR

8 SIMPLE STRATEGIES ON HOW TEENS CAN LEARN ENTREPRENEURIAL SKILLS AND LIVE HEALTHY

E. T. MULLONEY

CONTENTS

To Patrick, my ever-loving and supportive husband. You are the anchor of my life after God.

This book is dedicated to you, the unwavering source of love, support, and inspiration in my life. Your presence makes every page of our journey a beautiful story together with our fur baby Tiggy boy.

INTRODUCTION

You're scrolling through your Instagram feed, mindlessly double-tapping cute puppy videos and pics of delicious-looking food. Then a story catches your eye about an average teenager turned healthypreneur.

So, what's a healthypreneur, you ask? Well, it's not your typical teenage part-time job of flipping burgers or babysitting. It's a whole new ball game, where both hustle and health are involved, and success takes on a new meaning.

Let's take a look at the life of this healthypreneur. Just like you, Thomas had a regular life filled with school, sports, online gaming, and valuable time spent with his friends. But then he discovered the world of healthypreneurship—a fusion of being an entrepreneur while also maintaining a healthy, feel-good lifestyle.

Thomas had discovered his passion in life. He was no longer content with just cramming for exams and amusing himself with regular teenage pastimes during his free time. He found he had a passion for fitness, nutrition, and well-being.

He promoted his passion by starting to post-workout routines, meal prep hacks, and motivational quotes on social media. He was surprised when people actually started following him like crazy. In a very short time period, he managed to get a tribe of motivated teens rallying behind him, all eager to jump on the healthypreneur train.

Thomas decided that he also wanted to empower his friends to improve their lives. So, he further boosted his social media presence by organizing virtual fitness challenges, and he even launched his own line of sustainable workout gear.

Thomas got all this done by preaching balance. He certainly wasn't the type to burn the midnight oil and sacrifice sleep for success. He was smart enough to realize that real achievement comes from a blend of ambition and self-care. There's simply no point in working until you burn out, as you wouldn't be able to achieve anything else.

You see, healthypreneurship isn't just a trend. It can help you become the boss of your own life. You need to understand that success isn't worthwhile if you burn out and destroy your health in the process.

As a teenager, you're probably wondering how you can work toward a financially secure and fulfilling future. When you're young, you have big dreams of making money, but also of doing something you really enjoy, and that adds meaning to your life.

School doesn't really prepare one for becoming an entrepreneur, and this book will help you a great deal with your preparation.

In today's world, there are many opportunities, but it can be difficult to find the right guidance. We will help you develop much-needed entrepreneurial skills, while you also maintain a healthy lifestyle.

So, why should you read this book? What exactly is in it for you? Let's summarize its main benefits.

Firstly, this book will accompany you on a journey of empowerment. It's here to provide you with practical strategies, actionable insights, and a roadmap to becoming a healthypreneur—someone who not only excels in entre-preneurship but also prioritizes their health and well-being.

You're probably wondering what is the point of all this. In today's ever-changing and fast-evolving world, it's not just about making money; it's about making a meaningful impact on your life and those around you. You want to achieve financial stability, but without sacrificing your health and your relationships with others.

You could be wondering how this book is different from the books already out there. The answer is that it recognizes that as a teenager, you have unique needs, aspirations, and challenges, and it provides you with relatable practical advice.

The book will equip you with the knowledge, skills, and confidence to create your own unique path. You can seize your destiny and live life on your own terms.

But before we dive into the strategies that will help you become a healthypreneur, let's explore the main points and challenges that encourage you to buy this book.

You likely don't know that much about entrepreneurial education and healthy living. This book will help you understand entrepreneurship and healthy living. It will provide you with tips on how to choose a startup business wisely and how to manage your finances, all while maintaining a healthy lifestyle at the same time.

We will also look at the psychological and social aspects of financial decision-making. It will help you understand how important it is to make financially responsible decisions while also helping you deal with peer pressure and expectations. You'll be able to make smart financial choices without succumbing to overspending and peer pressure.

Fear of failure is one of the most important things you will have to overcome as an entrepreneur. We will guide you on how to embrace your failures as a valuable learning experience.

STRATEGY 1

UNLEASHING YOUR INNER HEALTHYPRENEUR AND THINKING LIKE A BOSS!

> *It's easy to be fooled by everyone's highlight reel or Instagram feed—business can look easy and flexible, but it's a really, really hard sport. Get ready for one of the hardest things you'll ever do but as someone who actually started a business at 14, it's totally worth it.*
>
> — TAJ PABARI, ASE GROUP CHIEF EXECUTIVE

Joe was a determined high school student who had an entrepreneurial vision and that set him aside from his peers. He had always wanted to work for himself and do something significant with his life, so at the age of 16 he decided to become a healthypreneur.

During his freshman year of high school, he noticed that his classmates were often stressed, sleep-deprived and struggling with their academic workload. He also felt the pressure to excel, but he refused to let it take over his life and decided to take matters into his own hands.

Joe invited his friends to his house one day after school, and they sat around, telling each other about how they were struggling with stress and staying focused in school. That gave him the idea to create a space where teenagers could find support and balance.

Joe started his journey to becoming a healthypreneur by doing research on stress management, mindfulness techniques, and the benefits of exercise for teenagers. Armed with all the knowledge he gathered, he created an after-school program.

His program focused on teaching his peers how to cope with stress and pressure in healthy ways. He organized weekly yoga and meditation sessions in the local park where he encouraged his friends and everyone else who joined to embrace mindfulness as a tool for personal growth. Eventually, he also organized workshops where he invited nutritionists and mental health experts to speak and provide insight to teenagers about holistic well-being.

He convinced his sister Melody to go into business with him, and he branched out his business to make and sell natural stress relief bath products. Melody was very enthusiastic about their business together, as she believed that self-care was an important part of well-being and she wanted her friends to also experience the benefits.

The word spread about Joe and Melody's business, and their turnover increased rapidly. They sold more and more products, and children from different schools started to attend their meetings and workshops. They were soon surrounded by a thriving community of like-minded individuals. Joe started to understand that they weren't only helping their peers but that they were also making connections and creating positive change.

Joe's journey wasn't without challenges. He had to balance his schoolwork and the demands of his growing business. At times he wondered if he had taken on too much, but his commitment to his vision kept him going. He understood how important it was to have balance in his life, and made sure he had time for self-care.

His hard work eventually paid off, and he received recognition from his school and the local community, his business even started receiving attention from regional media.

Like Joe, you too can be a successful healthypreneur, and we're going to look at some ways in which you can get started.

WHY HEALTHYPRENEURSHIP MATTERS FOR TEENS

Healthypreneurship might sound like a fancy word, but it's really a simple term to describe a unique form of success that is much needed in today's busy world since it is so focused on achievement. It's all about being smart, healthy, and ready for what's coming.

Starting and managing a business is an exciting journey, but it can also be demanding and stressful. You can easily find yourself caught up in non-stop workdays and sleepless nights. However, if you work this way for a long time, you can experience burnout both in your professional and private life. There are things you can do to maintain a balance between success and your overall well-being. We'll take a look at the essential habits shared by successful entrepreneurs who are able to maintain their momentum without sacrificing their health.

The Importance of Healthypreneurship at a Young Age

So, why is healthypreneurship so important for teenagers?

It teaches you to think outside the box and how to be a creative problem solver. You'll learn to think in new ways and come up with unique solutions to everyday problems. These skills will not only help you in your business, but also your everyday life. Critical thinking skills are often not taught in schools and we have to find ways to develop them on our own.

It helps get you into the right mindset to prepare for your future. It might feel to you like retirement is light years away, but it's really much closer than you think. You need to build a strong base to provide you with income in your golden years while you're still young and healthy enough to do so.

Healthypreneurship can help you understand money and how to make it work for you. It's like planting a tree now so that you can enjoy the fruits when you're older. Becoming a young entrepreneur will help you learn early on that making money isn't only about working hard for it, but also knowing about how to make money work for you. You'll learn the language of budgeting, investment, and building wealth.

You'll get a head start when it comes to managing your time and money, and before you know it, you'll be adulting before all your friends. You'll be the responsible one who can make all your own decisions.

It's also a way of future-proofing your life. The world is changing fast, and healthypreneurship will help you stay ahead of the rest. You'll learn how to adapt, bounce back from setbacks, and be strong when challenges come your way.

Stories of Successful Teenage Entrepreneurs Who Overcame Challenges

Young entrepreneurs have always been good at identifying opportunities and transforming them into successful businesses. Just consider Steve Jobs, who founded Apple and revolutionized technology in the twentieth century.

Let's take a look at a few more of these success stories.

The remarkable Kamaria Warren started her business when she was just seven years old. Kamaria and her mother, Shaunice Sasser, set out to find birthday invitations for Kamaria's upcoming party when they realized there were no products that represented Brown and Black girls (Lodge, 2019).

They got the idea to create Brown Girls Stationery. Kamaria, who is from McDonough, Georgia, began her mission to design party and school supplies, stationery, vegan purses, and accessories specifically tailored to girls like her. Her creations feature cheerful illustrations of Black and Brown girls, and she even started selling dolls.

At only 13 years old, Kamaria oversees a thriving business with five employees and five volunteers. She sells her products through various channels, including Shopify, Faire Marketplace, wholesale partnerships, and also at local events.

On average, her business sells an impressive 10,000 notebooks, 2,500 notepads, and 1,500 backpacks yearly. Kamaria also develops and expands her offerings. She has introduced 1,000 packs of party supplies and 1,000 new lip glosses and also releases a purse with an uplifting message every month.

Kamaria is motivated by the idea of seeing other girls wearing her creations and embracing their true selves. Her motto encapsulates her spirit: "Dear Brown girl, you have the ability to change the world."

Ryan Hickman, who is from Orange County, California, started his entrepreneurship journey when he was only three years old. He had always hated seeing bottles and other rubbish strewn on the ground, even when he was a small child, and he eventually decided that he wanted to do something about it.

Ryan started collecting items that could be recycled, and his dad took him to the local recycling center, where he received $5 for his efforts. This made him even more excited about recycling.

At only seven years old, he started his own business, named Ryan's Recycling Company. Ryan started receiving widespread attention. He received recognition from news organizations, including CNN Kid Wonder in 2017, and he also appeared on national TV shows like "Ellen" and "Today," where he shared his inspiring mission with the world.

Ryan sells t-shirts on his website that have messages like "Make the Sea Trash Free." He also supports the Pacific Marine Mammal Center with the proceeds of his sales and the income from his recycling efforts.

Not stopping there, Ryan also launched a nonprofit called Project 3R. The mission of this organization is to educate people of all ages worldwide about the importance of recycling and to coordinate community clean-up efforts. Ryan's message is that if a kid like him can contribute to changing the environmental situation, we can all do our part.

Moziah Bridges, from Memphis, is a stylish young entrepreneur. When he was nine years old, he struggled to find a bowtie to match his outfit. He decided to do something about this and started the popular business, Mo's Bows.

He started his business journey by learning how to sow. He made bowties from leftover fabric from his grandmother's sewing projects. As time progressed, he expanded his operations. He employed skilled tailors to handle the manufacturing while he focused on the creative and business aspects of Mo's Bows.

By the age of 20, Moziah Bridges had already achieved remarkable success and he specialized in meticulously crafted men's ties and accessories. He had the honor to present former President Barack Obama with a custom-made "Obama Blue" tie. His creations are also being sold by retailers like Cole Haan, Bloomingdale's, and Neiman Marcus.

Moziah also established the Go Mo Summer Camp Scholarship Fund, which sends underprivileged children from Memphis to summer camp. This also shows Moziah's commitment to making a positive impact beyond the world of fashion.

In the next chapter, we'll look at how effective time management can help you reach your goals.

HOW TO START YOUR FIRST BUSINESS WITH LIMITED FINANCIAL RESOURCES

Sarah was determined to start her own business, but she had only limited financial resources to help her do so. Her dream started to look impossible when she realized she would have to start her business with as little money as possible.

She knew she would have to be resourceful and come up with creative solutions that cost as little as possible. She couldn't rely on her parents to help her with money or bail out her business, as she knew they were also struggling financially.

We'll explore the practical steps and strategies that can help you kickstart your business on a shoestring budget. It's entirely possible to do it without breaking the bank. The path to entrepreneurial success begins with frugality, innovation, and unwavering determination.

Starting your first business with as little money as possible is a common goal for many young entrepreneurs. The following can help you get started on a limited budget.

Keeping Your Costs Down

Make sure you choose a business idea that doesn't require a substantial upfront investment. An online or service-based business will have lower startup costs than businesses that rely on physical products being sold. For example, if you don't have cash to develop products, but you're good at helping others and you have specialist knowledge on a certain subject such as math, it might be easier for you to advertise your services as an online tutor.

Creating a lean business plan can also help you keep your expenses in check. Develop a simplified business plan that outlines your business concept, target market, revenue model, and budget. Your plan should be focused and flexible.

Use your existing skills and resources. This could include using your own laptop, smartphone, or tools related to your business. If you have a laptop and internet connection, you may already have all the resources you require to start your online business.

Look for ways you can reduce your overhead costs. If you're working from home on your laptop, you shouldn't have that many overheads.

If you need someone to help you with something, such as creating content for your business website, consider outsourcing the work. It will save you money in the long term if you don't have to hire someone permanently to do the work for you. Who knows, maybe you'll even get the time and the motivation to learn the skills that will make it easier for you to do this type of work yourself in the future.

When it comes to marketing your services, it's possible to learn and implement basic marketing strategies yourself. You can also use free or low-cost online marketing tools, social media, and content marketing to reach your target audience.

Start small and grow your business gradually. Begin with a minimal viable product (MVP) to test the market. As your business gains support and starts making money, reinvest the profits to expand and improve your offerings.

If your business does provide products, negotiate with suppliers and service providers for discounts or better terms. You can also consider looking for crowdfunding platforms or small business grants that align with your business idea. This can give you additional funding without having to take loans.

Build a network of like-minded entrepreneurs who can provide advice and support, and potentially collaborate on projects, reducing costs and risks.

Be careful with your money. Prioritize spending on activities and resources that directly contribute to increasing your business number and growth. You should also keep on learning about affordable business practices.

Starting a business with little money requires creativity and resourcefulness. While it may be challenging, it's entirely possible to build a successful business if you plan carefully around your finances.

CHECKLIST OF SKILLS FOR YOUNG ENTREPRENEURS

To be a successful young entrepreneur, you need a combination of skills and abilities:

- You should be able to think outside the box, come up with innovative ideas, and solve problems creatively.
- Entrepreneurship often involves setbacks and failures. You need resilience, which involves the ability to bounce back from these and keep going.
- Effective communication is vital for pitching ideas, networking, and working with a team.
- As an entrepreneur, you'll likely be leading a team or project. Leadership skills will help you inspire and guide others.
- The business world is constantly changing, and you need to be able to adapt to this.
- Understanding budgets, cash flow, and financial planning is necessary for running a successful business.
- Good time management helps you prioritize tasks and be productive.
- Building relationships and networks can open doors and opportunities for your business.
- You need to be able to promote your product or service effectively.

- Entrepreneurs take risks, but they should be calculated risks. It's important to be able to understand risk and reward.
- In the digital age, having a basic understanding of technology and online tools is essential.
- You should focus on meeting the needs of your customers.
- You'll need to make important decisions quickly and effectively.
- Setting clear goals and working toward them is one of an entrepreneur's most important skills.
- Negotiating with partners, investors, or clients is a common part of entrepreneurship.
- You'll encounter many challenges, and problem-solving skills are critical.
- Understanding and managing your emotions, as well as those of others, is valuable in business relationships.
- Basic knowledge of business laws, contracts, and regulations is important.
- Understanding your target market and industry trends will help you make informed decisions.
- You can take acceptable risks, and you should always have a backup plan.

Entrepreneurship is also an ongoing learning experience. You can improve your abilities and skills as you gain experience and learn more in your field.

DEVELOPING ENTREPRENEURIAL ABILITIES WORKSHEET

This worksheet is designed to help you explore and develop your entrepreneurial abilities. Answering these questions can give you a better idea of the skills you already have and where you would still need to work on yourself. You can use the spaces provided below to answer them but if you need more space feel free to write in a notebook or use one of your digital devices.

Identify Your Passions

- List three things you are passionate about.

_____

_____

_____

- Could you turn your passions into potential business ideas?

_____

_____

_____

Innovative Thinking

- Think of a common problem in your community or school.

_____

_____

_____

- Brainstorm three solutions to this problem.

_____

_____

_____

Problem-Solving

- Recall a time when you faced a significant challenge.

_____

_____

_____

- Describe the challenge and how you overcame it.

_____

_____

_____

Identify Your Strengths and Weaknesses

- List three strengths you possess that would benefit an entrepreneur.

_____

_____

_____

- List three weaknesses on which you would want to improve.

_____

_____

_____

Business Ideas

- Create a list of ten business ideas that interest you. These can be creative ideas that would still need some work to refine them.

_____

_____

_____

- Highlight one idea that particularly appeals to you, and which your gut feeling tells you would be the right one for you.

_____

_____

_____

Market Research

- For the highlighted business idea, conduct basic market research.

_____

_____

- Who is your target audience? Is there a demand for your product or service?

_____

_____

_____

Networking

- Connect with someone who has experience as an entrepreneur or business leader. List your potential meetings below.

_____

_____

_____

- Ask them about their journey and any advice they can offer.

_____

_____

_____

Decision-Making

- Imagine you have to make a difficult decision regarding your business idea.

_____

_____

_____

- Write down your thought process for making this decision.

_____

_____

_____

Financial Awareness

- Calculate the startup costs for your business idea.

_____

_____

_____

- Create a simple budget for the first year of your business.

_____

_____

_____

_____

_____

_____

Presentation Skills

- Prepare a 2-minute pitch for your business idea. Write it below and then practice delivering it with enthusiasm.

_____

_____

_____

Continuous Learning

- Research a successful entrepreneur you admire. Summarize your research below.

_____

_____

_____

- What qualities or strategies have contributed to their success?

_____

_____

_____

Resilience

- Recall a setback you've faced in the past.

_____

_____

_____

- Describe how you overcame it and what you learned from the experience.

_____

_____

_____

Vision and Goals

- Define your long-term entrepreneurial vision.

_____

_____

_____

- Set three specific, achievable goals to work towards this vision.

_____

_____

_____

Action Plan

- Create an action plan outlining the steps you need to take to pursue your highlighted business idea.

Reflection

Write about what you've learned about yourself and your entrepreneurial abilities by completing this worksheet.

Entrepreneurship is an ongoing journey, and your abilities will continue to develop as you gain more experience and knowledge. Keep this worksheet and revisit it to keep track of your progress.

KEY TAKEAWAYS

- Healthypreneurship combines success with well-being.
- It teaches creative problem-solving and innovative thinking.
- It can prepare you for the future and the importance of managing money.
- It will empower you with early financial knowledge.
- It will help you develop your time and money management skills.
- Healthypreneurship can help you stay ahead in a fast-changing world.
- It will teach you adaptability, resilience, and strength in the face of challenges.

STRATEGY 2

CRUSH YOUR GOALS, RULE YOUR TIME

Your complaints, your drama, your victim mentality, your whining, your blaming, and all of your excuses have NEVER gotten you even a single step closer to your goals or dreams. Let go of your nonsense. Let go of the delusion that you DESERVE better and go EARN it! Today is a new day!

— STEVE MARABOLI

As the quote says, every day is full of endless opportunities that you need to get out there and earn. You've got big dreams, and there are lots of possibilities out there waiting for you. But there's one catch—you need a plan, a roadmap to turn those dreams into reality. Perhaps you've heard about goal setting, but you've never really tried it, because it just sounds like something that will bore you to death, so you've been winging it. This won't work In the long-term though, and you need to plan for success.

Don't worry, goal setting isn't about dull routines or boring to-do lists; it's your key to creating a successful and exciting life. It can actually be exciting to sculpt your dreams into achievable milestones.

We'll also introduce you to the SMART way of setting goals—Specific, Measurable, Achievable, Relevant, and Time-bound.

We'll also help you nurture your growth mindset. You can change challenges into opportunities to overcome your setbacks. They're all just stepping stones on your path to success.

GOAL SETTING

Imagine goal setting as a way of unlocking your talents. Without goals, we tend to go through life aimlessly, and we might never reach our full potential.

Tailored Techniques

You can choose from various goal-setting techniques that suit your style the best. Maybe you're someone who wants to visualize your goals or break them down into smaller steps. Let's take a look at some of these goal-setting techniques.

SMART Goals

This is one of the most popular and easiest techniques to use.

Specific: Be clear about what you want to achieve. For example, if you decide you want to be healthier, you need to set out specific ways in which you're going to achieve this such as deciding that you will follow a specific healthy diet plan and exercise for 30 minutes every day.

Measurable: You should be able to track your progress toward achieving your goals, for example, I will walk for 20 minutes every day.

Achievable: The goals you set for yourself should be achievable and realistic. For example, it's unrealistic to want to learn a new language in a week, but you could learn some basic phrases in a month.

Relevant: Your goals should align with your interests and values. If you love writing, a goal related to painting or drawing might be more relevant than something unrelated.

Time-bound: You need to set a deadline for your goals. The sense of urgency this creates will help you stay focused on achieving your goals. For example, this could be a specific date by which you're going to finish a school project.

Chunking Goals

This means breaking your big goals into smaller, manageable chunks. If you want to improve your grades, instead of aiming for an overall average increase right away, focus on getting better scores in one subject at a time.

Journaling

Record your goals and progress in a journal. Writing down your goals can make them feel more concrete, and it can motivate you to keep track of your progress.

Vision Boards and Mind Maps

Create a vision board with images and quotes that represent your goals and dreams. Place it where you can see it daily to stay motivated.

Creating a mind map is also a visual way to represent your goals, and it's useful for brainstorming and planning.

So, how do you create a mind map? Below is a simple sketch, but you can use different colors and pictures to make ideas stand out on your map.

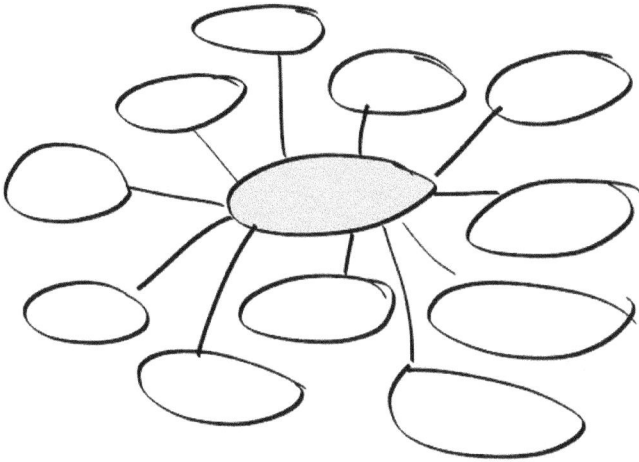

The basic idea of the mind map is as follows:

- Start your mind map with a central idea or topic in the center of the page.
- Draw main branches from the central idea to represent key categories or concepts related to the topic.
- Add subtopics as smaller branches extending from the main branches, that give specific details or ideas.
- Use keywords, short phrases, or simple images to represent ideas instead of long sentences.
- Connect related ideas with lines and arrows to show relationships and the flow of information.

- Organize the mind map hierarchically, placing the most important ideas at the top or center.
- Use colors, icons, or symbols to differentiate categories and highlight key points.
- Avoid clutter by focusing on capturing the main ideas and their connections.
- Review and refine the mind map to make sure it's logical and accurate.
- You can also do your mind mapping digitally on your computer or any of your digital devices.

Gamification

You can make it fun by turning your goals into a game with rewards and challenges. For each goal you achieve, treat yourself to something you enjoy.

Accountability Partner

Team up with a friend who has similar goals. You can motivate and support each other, and this can make the whole process more enjoyable.

Finally, you need to be flexible and willing to adjust your goals if needed. Your priorities can change, as life is often unpredictable.

Short-Term vs. Long-Term Goals

Short-term goals are like mini-missions. If you're an online game player, you'll know about the challenges your favorite character faces throughout the game.

Completing these mini-goals will also give you a sense of achievement and bring you closer to achieving your main goal.

You can see your long-term goals almost like the longer quests in your games, where you have to save your world from a villain. These are the big dreams you want to achieve, and they require time and dedication.

So, why both short-term and long-term goals? It's like having a game with different levels. You can't jump straight to the final level, you need to pass the earlier stages first. Short-term goals prepare you for the epic battles ahead!

EFFECTIVE TIME MANAGEMENT

Effective time management is a valuable skill that can benefit you in various aspects of your life, from your schoolwork to extracurricular activities and personal goals. You should implement the following practical tips:

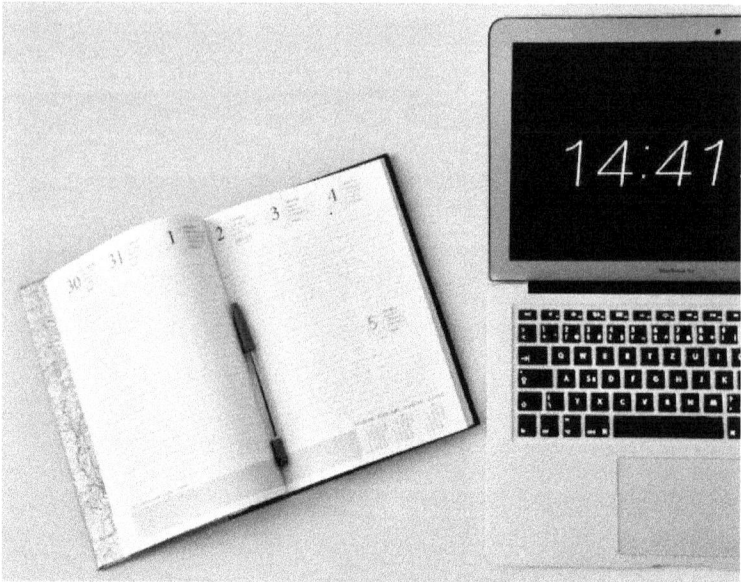

Set Reminders For Your Tasks

As a teenager, your life can get pretty hectic with school, sports, social activities, and more. You could find that you easily forget about important tasks or deadlines. If you have a smartphone or a digital planner, use it to set reminders for your homework assignments, project due dates, and even your chores like doing the dishes, or taking out the laundry. This way, you won't miss out on anything important, and you'll feel more in control of your responsibilities.

Create a Daily Planner

A daily planner, whether it's a physical notebook or a digital app, can help you solve the puzzle of your daily life, and keep your wits together. It's only too easy to become overwhelmed when you have many things going at once. Write down everything you need to do, including schoolwork, practice sessions, and even your times for relaxation and socialization. Plan your day the night before or in the morning to give you a clear roadmap, and to make sure that you do everything that's important.

Set Time Limits For Tasks

Avoid spending too much time on your assignments or becoming distracted by assigning specific time limits to your tasks. For instance, if you have an English assignment, tell yourself you'll work on it for 30 minutes, take a short break, and then work on it for another 30 minutes. This will make your tasks more manageable and will prevent you from procrastinating.

Block Out Distractions

You may find it challenging to stay focused, especially with social media, games, and other digital temptations. Set "focus" times where you turn off notifications or use apps that block distracting websites. This will help you concentrate on your tasks and complete them more efficiently.

Establish a Routine

Developing a daily routine can change your life. It not only helps you manage your time better but also creates a sense of stability. Set aside specific times for studying, exercising, socializing, and relaxation. Over time, your routine will become a habit, and it will help you manage your time more effectively.

Prioritize Your Tasks

You need to prioritize your tasks. Some will always be more important than others, and you should focus on the urgent ones first. You will also have to learn to say no and to prioritize and find a balance between your commitments. If you say yes to everything, you'll just become overwhelmed. Being selective about the activities and responsibilities you take on ensures you have enough time for your priorities.

Effective time management is a skill that takes practice. It's okay to make adjustments along the way as you figure out what works best for you. Implementing these tips and staying committed to managing your time wisely will help you excel in your studies, pursue your passions, and maintain balance in your life.

Exercises and Activities to Help You Adopt a Growth Mindset

Developing a growth mindset as a teenager can help you when it comes to your personal and academic development.

So, what is the difference between a growth and a fixed mindset?

If you have a fixed mindset, you believe that your abilities, talents, and intelligence are things that you were born with and that they can't change. You might think that if you're not good at something, you'll never be good at it. For example, if you're struggling with a certain subject at school, you don't believe that you'll ever be able to improve at this subject.

If you have a fixed mindset, you'll probably avoid challenges because you'll be afraid of making mistakes. You might give up easily when things get tough because you believe you can't improve.

In a growth mindset, you believe that your abilities, talents, and intelligence are not fixed and that you can develop them with time and effort. For example, you enjoy drawing and art, but you realize and accept that you will have to put a lot of work into it if you want to pursue this as a career on a professional level.

The following activities and exercises can help you develop a growth mindset.

Think About Your Mindset

Consider the difference between a fixed and a growth mindset. Ask yourself questions about your abilities and intelligence:

- Have you ever thought that you're not good at something and that you'll never be?
- Do you think you can learn and improve at something if you put in the effort?
- Which mindset do you think you have?

Embrace Mistakes and Failures

If you want to develop a growth mindset, you have to be able to accept your failures and mistakes.

- Think about a recent mistake or failure you experienced, whether at school or in your personal life.
- What did you learn from the experience? Did it help you improve?
- Share your story with your friends to normalize that making mistakes is a normal part of learning and growing up.

Look For Challenges

Developing a growth mindset involves looking for challenges and new experiences that will help you grow as a person.

- Start taking part in an activity you've never tried before, like coding, a new sport, or a different style of art.
- Step out of your comfort zone and persevere, even in situations where you're experiencing difficulties.
- Write in a journal to keep track of your progress and the skills you acquire along the way.

Visualize Your Growth

Visualization can help you develop a growth mindset.

- Imagine a skill or subject you struggle with, like math or perhaps playing a certain sport.
- Visualize yourself gradually getting better at it. Imagine all the small steps you take to get better.
- Create a vision board or journal where you document your progress over the weeks or months.

Learn From Your Role Models

It can be inspiring to learn from role models who have a growth mindset.

- You should do research and choose a role model—whether it's a famous person, a teacher, or a family member—who has overcome challenges through their growth mindset.
- Study how they overcome obstacles and challenges.
- Let their experiences motivate you when you're facing your own challenges.

Encourage Positive Self-Talk

Positive self-talk can help you develop a growth mindset, in the following ways:

- You should pay attention to your self-talk, and challenge negative self-talk.
- Replace negative self-talk with positive affirmations such as a belief that you can learn and improve.
- Create a list of positive statements, and read them whenever you need a boost. Put them up somewhere in your home where it will be easy for you to see them.

Set Growth-Oriented Goals

As you know by now, goal setting is an important part of your personal growth.

- You need to set specific, achievable goals for yourself, whether they are related to academics, hobbies, or personal development.
- Break your goals down into smaller, more manageable goals.
- Celebrate your progress along the way, as you get closer to achieving your goal.

Embrace Feedback

Constructive feedback is important for your growth. Listen to the feedback you receive from your teachers, coaches, or peers on your work or performance. See it as an opportunity to learn and improve, rather than as criticism.

Sarah's SMART Success Journey

Sarah was a determined and ambitious teenager with a passion for fashion. At sixteen, she had a vision of creating her own sustainable fashion brand. However, she knew that turning her dream into a reality would require more than just ambition and that she would need to set some goals. She decided to use the SMART strategy to do so.

S - Specific

Her first goal was to be specific about her business idea. She wanted her fashion brand to focus on eco-friendly, handmade clothing. She aimed to promote sustainability and ethical fashion practices. Sarah spent hours researching sustainable materials, production processes, and suppliers. She ensured that all the details aligned with her vision.

M - Measurable

Sarah knew she needed a way to measure her progress, as she would likely be successful sooner if she followed this process. She set targets for herself, such as designing and creating her first line of products within six months. Sarah also tracked the number of garments she produced and the materials she used. This helped her to assess her progress and adjust her goals accordingly.

A - Achievable

Sarah also decided to break her main goal down into smaller, achievable steps. She started by learning the basics of sewing and design, attending workshops, and connecting with local artisans who shared her passion. She was determined to make her brand unique, which meant learning about sustainable production techniques and marketing strategies. All these steps took her closer to achieving her ultimate goal.

R - Relevant

Sarah ensured that her goals were relevant to her vision. She constantly asked herself if her actions were contributing to the success of her sustainable fashion brand. This helped her stay focused on what truly mattered, and she didn't get distracted by anything that could derail her.

T - Time-Bound

Time was of the utmost importance to Sarah. She knew that setting deadlines was crucial. Her SMART goals included launching her brand's website within a year, gaining her first 100 customers within 18 months, and turning a profit by the end of her second year in business. She kept working towards these deadlines and kept adjusting her goals as needed.

This wasn't easy. There were moments of doubt, late nights, and inevitable setbacks. But Sarah's SMART goals kept her on track and motivated.

Two years later, Sarah's sustainable fashion brand was flourishing. Her brand was not only a financial success but a symbol of hope for a more sustainable and ethical fashion industry.

SELF-GUIDED ACTIVITY TO SET SMART GOALS

This activity will help you set SMART goals independently. You can use the spaces provided below to answer them but if you need more space feel free to write in a notebook or use one of your digital devices.

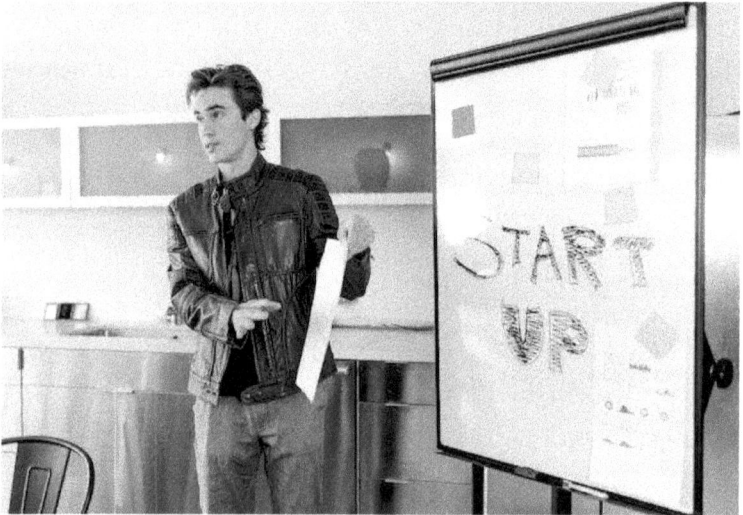

Begin by writing notes on the importance of setting SMART goals for personal development, academic success, and future planning.

Definition of SMART goals. Before you begin setting your SMART goals, you need to understand the definitions:

- **Specific:** Goals should be clear and well-defined.
- **Measurable:** Goals should include criteria to track progress.

- **Achievable:** Goals should be realistic and within reach.
- **Relevant:** Goals should align with their interests and values.
- **Time-bound:** Goals should have a set deadline for completion.

Jot down at least three goals for yourself. These can be related to education, personal development, hobbies, or any aspect of life that is important to you.

Choose one of your goals and analyze it using the SMART criteria. Use the following questions to guide you:

- **Specific:** What is your goal? Can you make it more specific?

_____

_____

_____

- **Measurable:** How will you measure your progress? What criteria will you use?

_____

_____

- **Achievable:** Is this goal realistic given your current resources and constraints?

_____

_____

_____

- **Relevant:** Why is this goal important to you? How does it align with your values?

_____

_____

_____

- **Time-bound:** When do you want to achieve this goal?

_____

_____

_____

If you choose to use a notebook (whether physical or digital) find a fresh page where you can write your selected goal and create a table with the headings: Specific, Measurable, Achievable, Relevant, and Time-bound. Fill in each column with the answers you would have received from your analysis. You can do the same for the questions below.

Visualize Success: Visualize yourself successfully achieving your goal. What does it look and feel like?

_____

_____

_____

Action Plan: Create a basic action plan for your goal. What steps will you take to work toward it? Can you overcome potential obstacles?

_____

_____

_____

Reflection: Reflect on how setting SMART goals makes you feel.

_____

_____

_____

Regular Review: Regularly review and adjust your goals as needed and track your progress in your notebook or the space provided below.

_____

_____

_____

_____

_____

_____

KEY TAKEAWAYS

- Goals are essential for turning your dreams into reality.
- Goal setting is exciting and not just about dull routines.
- SMART goals (Specific, Measurable, Achievable, Relevant, Time-bound) are a very effective way of setting your goals.
- Tailored techniques for goal setting include visualization, chunking, journaling, vision boards, and mind maps.
- Be flexible and adapt your goals to your changing priorities in life.

- Short-term goals are like mini-missions, leading to a sense of achievement.
- Long-term goals are like longer, epic quests, and you need to be dedicated to achieve them.
- Short-term goals prepare you for long-term success.
- Use reminders for your tasks and create a daily planner.
- Set time limits for tasks to prevent procrastination. If we don't have deadlines or time limits, it will usually take us much longer to complete certain tasks.
- Block out distractions and establish a daily routine.
- Prioritize tasks and learn to say no when necessary.
- Effective time management is a skill that you can improve with practice. It will set you ahead of the rest if you learn these skills at a young age.
- If you have a fixed mindset, you believe you were born with your skills and talents, and you can't do anything to change them. If you have a growth mindset, you believe you can keep on learning and improve your skills throughout your life.
- You should regard mistakes and failures as opportunities for learning. Don't get depressed by them, just keep on going.
- Seek out challenges and new experiences.

- Make sure you surround yourself with role models with a growth mindset. You can learn a lot from these positive people.
- Encourage positive self-talk and replace negative thoughts. As soon as you realize you're starting to think in a negative way, work on changing your thoughts.
- Set growth-oriented goals, break them into smaller steps, and celebrate your progress.
- Embrace constructive feedback as a tool for improvement.

In the next chapter, we look at how you can energize your body and supercharge your brain.

STRATEGY 3

ENERGIZE YOUR BODY AND SUPERCHARGE YOUR BRAIN

> *The human body, like the human mind, is best at versatility and adaptability. This is our greatest skill and our greatest chance to unlock natural potential. What that means in terms of physical movement is that a fairly equal amount of time and effort should be allocated to the widest possible range of activity. That includes strength, flexibility, precision, and endurance, but it certainly doesn't stop there.*
>
> — DARRELL CALKINS

As the quote says, your body and your mind are versatile and adaptable. It's not just a tool for lifting stuff or running around; it's a finely tuned machine that can do so much more. That's your secret weapon, and in this chapter, we're going to unleash its full potential.

You see, it's not just about being strong or flexible. It's about being an all-rounder, a dynamic force to be reckoned with.

So, what's the deal? It's not just about pumping iron or mastering yoga poses. It's about exploring the wide world of physical movement. You're going to discover strength, flexibility, precision, and endurance, but guess what? We're not stopping there. We're delving into the vast spectrum of what your body can achieve. Get ready to unlock your full physical potential and become a true champion of versatility.

DISCOVERING THE MIND-BODY CONNECTION

There's a strong connection between your physical and mental health. If you feel better, you'll think better too. So, you can say a healthy body is your secret weapon to developing superthinking powers.

Your mind and body are two sides of the same coin. What happens on one side will influence the other one. When you're physically fit, your mind will be sharper and you'll be better equipped to tackle challenges.

Stress is a part of life, and in your case, it's probably the result of schoolwork, exams, and social pressures. But here's the twist—when your body is in good shape, you'll also be able to handle stress more efficiently. Exercise, a healthy diet, and enough sleep act will bust your stress and help your mind stay cool under pressure.

Exercise isn't just for muscles; it's for your brain too. Physical activity increases blood flow to the brain, which makes your brain work better. It's almost like giving it a power boost.

Exercise triggers the release of "feel-good hormones" endorphins, which can lift your mood. A healthy body can help you deal with your teenage years with more resilience.

Your mind and body both benefit from a healthy diet. A balanced diet, rich in essential nutrients, supports optimal brain function. Quality sleep also helps you concentrate and learn better.

A healthy mind also supports your physical well-being. When you're mentally strong, you'll also be more likely to make choices that are better for your body.

Diet, Exercise, and Sleep

Sleep might not be the first thing on your mind, but it's important for a successful and healthy life. Your teenage years are a whirlwind of changes and experiences, and getting the right amount of quality sleep can make a massive difference.

Diet and Sleep

Think of your body as a car that needs the right fuel to run smoothly. A balanced diet with plenty of fruits, veggies, whole grains, and lean proteins is like premium gasoline for your system. Spicy and sugary foods should be avoided close to bedtime, as they can give you indigestion and disrupt your sleep.

While it's important to stay hydrated, you should monitor your fluid intake in the evening to prevent nighttime trips to the bathroom. You need to find the right balance as dehydration can also disturb your sleep.

Love your caffeine and sugary snacks? They can be your buddies during the day, but late afternoon or evening caffeine and sugar can linger in your system and keep you tossing and turning at night. Avoid these treats before you go to bed.

Try to establish a regular eating schedule and stick to it as much as possible. Regularity helps regulate your internal body clock, making it easier to fall asleep and wake up.

Exercise and Sleep

Exercise doesn't only help you keep your weight down, it will also help you sleep better. Physical activity during the day can help you fall asleep faster and also sleep deeper. So, get out there and start moving around. Exercise doesn't have to be a punishment, it can be something you enjoy, such as dancing.

Exercise boosts your adrenaline and energy, so don't do too much right before you go to bed. Complete your workout at least a few hours before sleep to give your body a chance to wind down.

A consistent exercise routine can help you improve your sleep quality. Find an activity you love and stick with it by making it a part of your regular routine.

Sunlight plays an important role in regulating your body's internal clock. Outdoor activities, especially in the morning, can help synchronize your circadian rhythms and promote better sleep.

It's not about making drastic changes overnight. Small adjustments can improve your sleep quality, which will make sure you have more energy and a brighter outlook on life.

Your teenage years are about self-discovery and growth, and you need quality sleep and energy to get the most from your energy. So, eat well, move often, and sleep tight.

GOOD WAYS TO RECHARGE

You can give your body the TLC it deserves in the following ways.

Spend Time in Nature

Try to spend as much time as possible in nature, as this can also be your escape from a stressful life. Take a break, go for a hike, sit by a lake, or take a walk in the park. The fresh air and greenery can clear your mind and lift your spirits.

Keep a Gratitude Journal

Keep a journal and write about the things for which you're grateful in your life. Write down the good stuff—a friendly chat with great friends, a tasty meal, or even just a sunny day. It can boost your mood and remind you of all the positive things in your life.

Expand Your Consciousness

Feed your curiosity. Read, and watch documentaries, or podcasts on topics that interest you. Expand your horizons and explore the world beyond your immediate surroundings. This is especially important for your personal growth and development throughout your life.

Meditate

Meditation isn't just for monks; it's for anyone who wants a clear mind. Take a few minutes to sit quietly, breathe deeply, and let go of stress. Your brain will feel refreshed.

Express Yourself Creatively

It doesn't have to be perfect, it's just about finding a way to express yourself. Whether it's painting, short story writing, or playing music, get creative. It will be a helpful outlet for your emotions and thoughts.

Treat Your Body Like a Temple

Your body needs to last for your entire lifetime, so treat it as well as you possibly can. Eat a balanced diet, get enough sleep, and drink plenty of water. Your future self will thank you for these healthy habits.

Start a Mindful Morning Routine

Mornings will set the tone for the rest of your day. Start with a healthy breakfast where you allow yourself a chance to quietly think about your intentions for the rest of the day. It can help you feel grounded and ready to take on challenges.

Regularly Learn Something New

Your learning doesn't have to be limited to the classroom. Learning keeps your mind agile and can open the doors to exciting opportunities. The new skills you learn can even lead to business opportunities.

Volunteer

Helping others can be a powerful way to recharge if you give your time to something you're passionate about. The satisfaction of making a difference can boost your self-esteem and well-being.

LIVING THE HEALTHY LIFE: ALEX'S STORY

Alex was a high school student and aspiring entrepreneur with big dreams. He was passionate about technology, and he had recently launched his own startup, which designs innovative apps to make people's lives easier.

Alex's days were filled with excitement, challenges, and countless new ideas. His journey was a whirlwind of online meetings, brainstorming sessions, and coding marathons. On top of that, he still needed to do his schoolwork. It seemed like there was never enough time in the day to tackle everything on his to-do list.

He often didn't get enough sleep, as he felt this was the only way he could get more hours into his hectic, busy days. His startup's success was his top priority, and he believed that sacrificing a few hours of sleep each night was a small price to pay for his dreams. However, his friends and family were worried. They knew that something had to change.

One evening, Alex's best friend, Sarah, invited him to a local park for a chat. They sat down on a bench and she told him about her concerns. She told him that she admired his dedication, but that he also needed to take care of his health by sleeping more. Sarah said that he was starting to appear worn out and anxious.

Alex told her that he had so much to do that he simply couldn't afford to sleep a full 8 hours every night.

Sarah told him that he could start by making small changes and that a well-rested mind is more creative and efficient.

Alex decided to take Sarah's advice seriously, as he had also started to get worn out and had recently noticed that he was getting more sick than ever before. He began to prioritize his sleep by establishing a bedtime routine. He turned off his phone and computer an hour before bedtime, opting for a relaxing book instead. He started going to bed and waking up at the same time every day, ensuring he got at least 7 hours of sleep. It took a while, but he finally started seeing the positive effects of his changed routine.

As Alex started sleeping better, he noticed a remarkable change in his work. His mind was sharper, and he could think more clearly. His coding became more efficient, and he came up with innovative solutions faster than ever before. He even found more time for exercise, which gave him the energy to tackle each day's challenges.

With improved sleep habits, Alex's startup began to thrive. Investors were impressed by his creativity and energy, and the quality of his work improved. Alex realized that Sarah was right all along—sleep was a game-changer for his business journey.

His story also encouraged his friends with entrepreneurial ambitions to prioritize their sleep. They learned that quality sleep wasn't a hindrance but could actually help them achieve their dreams earlier.

WORKSHEET: DISCOVER YOUR MIND-BODY CONNECTION

Complete the following exercises to discover your mind-body connection. Find a quiet, comfortable space to focus and reflect.

Start your journey by keeping a Mind-Body journal. Create a two-column table in your journal or on a blank piece of paper. Label the first column "Mental" and the second column "Physical."

In the "Mental" column, jot down any thoughts, emotions, or stressors you've experienced recently. For example, you might write that you feel stressed about exams, or anxious when you have to do a presentation in class.

In the "Physical" column, write down how you have experienced these factors in your body. Are there any physical sensations associated with these thoughts or emotions? For example, you could have stomach pains or a tight chest when you feel stressed.

Breathing Exercise

Practice deep breathing to feel the connection between your breath and your state of mind. Close your eyes, sit up straight, and take a deep breath in through your nose for a count of four. Hold for a count of two, and then exhale through your mouth for a count of six. Pay attention to how your body and mind feel before and after this exercise.

Body Scan Meditation

Sit or lie down somewhere it's quiet. Close your eyes and focus your attention on different parts of your body, starting from your toes and moving up to your head. As you focus on each body part, notice any tension, discomfort, or sensations. Be aware of how your mental state may be affecting your body.

Emotion Check-In

Reflect on your most common emotions throughout the day. Are you frequently stressed, anxious, happy, or relaxed? Write your emotions down. Try to identify patterns in your emotional states and see if they agree with specific physical symptoms.

Physical Activity

Engage in a physical activity of your choice, like a short workout, yoga, or a walk. While doing this, pay attention to how your physical activity affects your mood. How do you feel after exercising compared to before?

Gratitude Journal

Write down three things you're grateful for today. Reflect on how this exercise makes you feel both mentally and physically. Do you notice any changes in your body when you focus on gratitude?

_____

_____

_____

_____

_____

Reflection

- How do your thoughts and emotions impact your physical well-being?

_____

_____

_____

- How does your physical health affect your mental state?

_____

_____

_____

- Can you identify any patterns in the mind-body connection through this exercise?

_____

_____

_____

- Are there any actions you can take to improve this connection for your overall well-being?

_____

_____

_____

Action Plan

Based on your reflections, write down a simple action plan. What steps can you take to strengthen your mind-body connection and promote better health? This will include stress management techniques, regular exercise, mindfulness practices, or seeking support when needed.

_____

_____

_____

_____

_____

Regular Check-Ins

Check in regularly with your mind and body connection. Make a point of regularly reviewing your journal entries.

A LIFELONG LEARNING MENTALITY

If you have a lifelong learning mentality, also known as a growth mindset, you follow a psychological and intellectual approach to life where you focus on gaining knowledge and skills throughout your life. A lifelong learning mentality has certain key characteristics.

People who have a lifelong learning mentality are naturally curious and eager to explore new ideas, concepts, and experiences. They're always interested in learning new things, and will even learn new skills from watching programs on YouTube.

They can also embrace change and view challenges as opportunities to learn and grow, rather than as setbacks. If you overreact to every challenge in your life, you run the risk of getting caught up in a victim mentality, and you could start believing that you're not capable of doing anything.

You need to be open to different perspectives and willing to consider new viewpoints, even if they conflict with your existing beliefs. You recognize your strengths and weaknesses, and this helps you recognize areas in your life where you still need to make improvements. You're committed to becoming a better version of yourself.

You're open to receiving feedback and you seek guidance from mentors or experts in your field.

A lifelong learning mentality also consists of informal learning, skill acquisition, personal development, and a mindset that encourages growth and self-discovery throughout one's life.

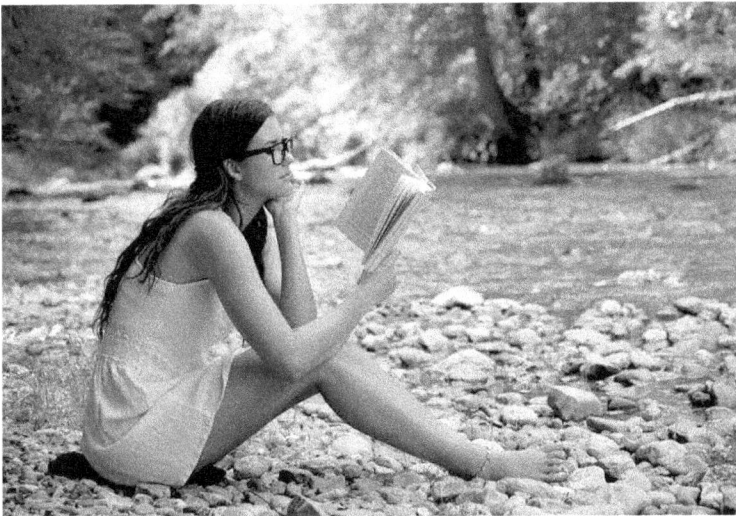

Cassandra's Lifelong Journey to Success

Cassandra, a dynamic and driven entrepreneur, understood that the key to achieving success in the ever-evolving world of business was a lifelong commitment to learning. From a young age, she believed in continuous education and self-improvement, which helped her build a successful business.

Cassandra's entrepreneurial journey began when she launched her tech startup at the age of 16. She was passionate about creating innovative software solutions, but she also knew that the technology landscape was constantly changing. She had a vision for her company, but she also recognized that it was essential to stay ahead of the curve.

Embracing Change

Cassandra knew that technology was a field where change was the only constant. She not only embraced change but actively sought it out. She stayed updated with the latest industry trends, attended conferences, and read research papers. This allowed her to pivot her business when necessary and adapt to new technologies and methodologies.

Networking

Cassandra understood the value of networking. She built a strong professional network by attending industry events and engaging with experts in her field. These connections provided her with insights, mentorship, and collaborative opportunities that were instrumental in her business growth.

Formal Education

Cassandra didn't stop with her initial degree. She pursued additional formal education through online courses, workshops, and certifications. She even encouraged her team to do the same. Her business benefited from the collective knowledge and expertise of her educated workforce.

Experimentation and Innovation

Cassandra fostered a culture of experimentation and innovation within her company. She encouraged her team to try new ideas and technologies, allowing them to learn from their mistakes and successes. This culture of innovation helped her business stay competitive and ahead of the curve.

Feedback and Adaptation

Cassandra actively sought feedback from her clients, team, and mentors. She used this feedback to refine her business strategies and improve her products. This commitment to ongoing improvement was a driving force behind her company's success.

Resilience

Despite the inevitable challenges and setbacks in business, Cassandra remained resilient. She saw failures as opportunities for learning and growth, and she shared these experiences with her team to inspire a culture of resilience and adaptability.

Over the years, Cassandra's company grew into a renowned tech firm, known for its innovative solutions and adaptable approach. Her commitment to lifelong learning created a dynamic and agile business that thrived in a rapidly changing landscape. She also became a mentor to other aspiring entrepreneurs, sharing her wisdom and emphasizing the importance of continual education and growth.

Cassandra's story serves as a powerful reminder that a lifelong learning mentality is not just a personal philosophy; it's a powerful strategy for success in today's dynamic business world. Her journey highlights the transformative impact of staying curious, open to new ideas, and committed to personal and professional growth.

KEY TAKEAWAYS

- Your body and mind are versatile and adaptable.
- Focus on being an all-rounder in terms of physical movement.

- You should explore strength, flexibility, precision, endurance, and more to unleash your full potential.
- Your physical and mental health are interconnected.
- Physical fitness sharpens your mind and helps you tackle challenges.
- If you have a healthy body, you'll be better able to manage stress, it will boost your mood and support better decision-making.
- Quality sleep is important during your teenage years, as you're still developing physically and emotionally.
- A balanced diet with regular eating patterns will fuel your body.
- You should avoid caffeine and sugary snacks should be avoided near bedtime.
- Exercise helps you sleep better and should be a regular part of your routine.
- Sunlight and outdoor activities will help regulate your body's internal clock.
- Spending time in nature can reduce your stress levels.
- Maintaining a gratitude journal can boost your mood.
- Expand your consciousness through reading and exploration.
- Practice meditation for a clear mind.

- Expressing yourself creatively can help you with emotional regulation.
- Prioritize self-care and healthy habits.
- Continue learning beyond the classroom. People with a lifelong learning mentality often have the most meaningful lives.
- Volunteering can also give you a sense of fulfillment and well-being.

In the next chapter, we will look at entrepreneurship and how you can create your own unique healthypreneurial path with confidence and purpose.

STRATEGY 4

THE TEEN ENTREPRENEUR'S TOOLBOX

If you've got an idea, start today. There's no better time than now to get going. That doesn't mean quit your job and jump into your idea 100% from day one, but there's always small progress that can be made to start the movement.

— KEVIN SYSTROM, INSTAGRAM

So, what exactly is this "entrepreneurship" thing, and why should you, as a teenager, care about it? A good way to think of it is as the ultimate adventure in creativity, innovation, and problem-solving. You identify a problem, find a solution, and then take the initiative to make it happen. You may think this journey is only for adults, but you can also be an entrepreneur.

Let's take a more in-depth look at what it means to be an entrepreneur.

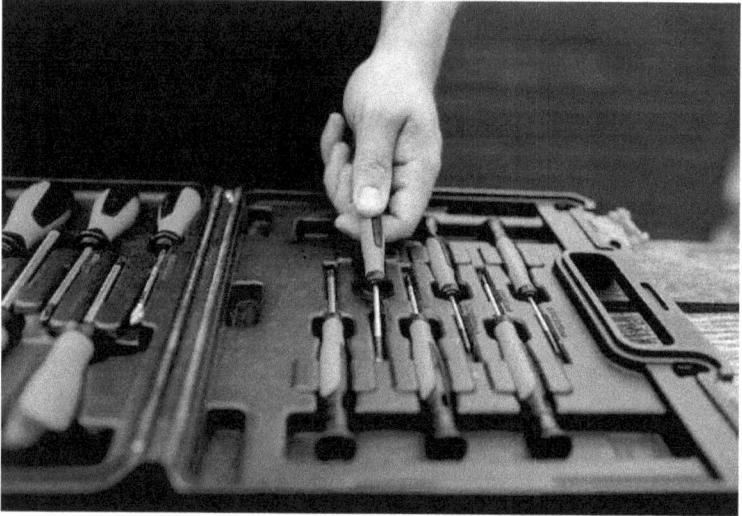

ENTREPRENEURSHIP: WHAT IT'S ALL ABOUT

Entrepreneurs are problem solvers. They spot issues, both big and small, and come up with smart and innovative ways to fix them. Business owners need to be able to think outside the box, so their imaginations are often their most important tool. They need to be able to dream big and bring fresh ideas to the table.

It's a huge responsibility because as a business owner you need to work out your own way in which you will achieve success. The answers aren't always in books, and you can't always rely on adults to provide you with the answers you're looking for. You need to step up and take charge of making your dreams a reality.

Keep looking for better ways to do things, and make sure you stay up to date with the latest ways of doing things. Push the boundaries. To be a successful entrepreneur, you need to be able to adapt and evolve.

Entrepreneurs are usually hands-on. It's not only about being book smart. You learn by doing, taking calculated risks, and even embracing failure as a stepping stone to success. Your mistakes are simply learning opportunities.

Being an entrepreneur isn't limited to a specific age group. It's a mindset that will empower you to shape your future and make a mark on the world.

Why Teenagers Should Become Entrepreneurs

So, why should you start as a teenager?

You're bursting with creativity, and you likely have lots of fresh ideas. Even though you don't have all the knowledge you need yet, you have tons of energy and you want to do things differently. You also don't have as many responsibilities as older entrepreneurs who may have to balance their work and family life and can focus most of your attention on your business, except for your school work.

Entrepreneurship gives you the practical life experience you need, as you learn by doing. It's an opportunity to learn practically, instead of just theory from textbooks and lectures. You can learn by taking action.

You don't have to wait until you're older and have completed your education to make a difference. As a teen-preneur, you can start making your mark on the world right now. Your ideas have the power to solve problems, inspire change, and leave a legacy. The challenges that come with being a young entrepreneur also help you build your resilience. After all, you can only survive as an entrepreneur if you're able to bounce back from challenges and face them head-on.

Entrepreneurship can also be a good fit for you if you want independence and freedom. You can be the boss and set your own goals, make your own decisions, and enjoy the freedom to work when and where you want. Just make sure that you're always open to learning from others when they offer you useful advice. Being the boss doesn't mean that you know everything and you should keep on learning to improve your business.

You could end up discovering your true passion in life through entrepreneurship. We often don't know what we want until we try different things. Entrepreneurship can be like a journey of self-discovery, as it helps you find out what you really care about.

Being a teenpreneur can give you the opportunity to connect to people who can help you get further in life. You'll build a network of mentors, peers, and supporters who can guide you along the way. These connections can be valuable for you throughout your life and can help you build your business.

THE ADVANTAGES AND DISADVANTAGES OF BEING AN ENTREPRENEUR

Like with everything in life, there are advantages and disadvantages to being an entrepreneur. Let's go through them together so you can decide for yourself if you think the pros outweigh the cons.

+ *The Pros*

There are many pros to being an entrepreneur, and once you're on this journey, you won't want to look back.

Freedom and Independence

Entrepreneurs can set their own schedules and decide how and when they want to work. For example, if you love photography, you can start your own photography business and choose when and where to take photos. People can hire you to take photos at events, and you can structure your time in a way that suits you best.

Creative Expression

You can use entrepreneurship as a canvas for your creativity. For example, if you make a unique range of clothes, you can start your own online art store, and showcase and sell your unique creations to a global audience. You could do the same with any other artistic item and you have the creative freedom to express yourself through your work.

Learning From Your Mistakes

Every setback in your business is a valuable lesson. It might be difficult to see this at first, but every time something goes wrong there's an opportunity for you to learn more and not make the same mistake again. For example, you have a business where you make healthy food and deliver it to people. You have a small delivery vehicle, and you have to learn the ins and outs as you go. However, your mistakes in the kitchen become opportunities to improve your recipes and customer service.

Leaving Your Mark

Healthypreneurship gives you the chance to leave your mark on the world. For example, you start a company that provides clean drinking water to poor communities. Your business is changing lives and leaving a lasting legacy of positive change.

Flexibility

When you're an entrepreneur, you don't have to follow a nine-to-five schedule. You have the flexibility to work when and where you want. This is brilliant for teenagers who are still at school, as you can structure your business ventures around your learning time. Your office is basically wherever you connect to the internet. For example, you can share quick blog updates while waiting for your friends in a restaurant, or squeeze in some work between doing your homework.

Potential for Unlimited Earnings

Unlike a regular office job, there's no limit to what you can earn. For example, you could create a new app that becomes a massive hit and provides you with substantial income. The harder you work and the more value you can provide to people, the more money you will earn.

Pursuit of Passion

Entrepreneurship allows you to turn your passion into a profession. If you're an animal lover, you can start a pet-sitting or dog-walking business. If you love children, you could become a babysitter. You get to spend your time doing whatever it is you love, and making money from it.

Control and Decision-Making

You have complete control over your business and you can make decisions that align with your vision. For example, if you want to sell eco-friendly products, you can start a business dedicated to sustainable, environmentally conscious goods. Product development, marketing, and company values are all your decisions.

Networking Opportunities

As an entrepreneur, you have the chance to connect with people from various backgrounds. Let's say you're an aspiring fashion designer, with a passion for exercise gear and you want to promote good health. By starting your fashion brand, you can work with models, photographers, and content creators who can help you promote your range. In this way, you will expand your network and learn from different experts in the industry.

Leaving a Legacy

The business you build can be a legacy for your family. A successfully owned family business that can be passed down to your children, providing them with a secure future.

— *The Cons*

Before you set out on your journey to start your business, there are certain disadvantages you have to keep in mind.

Uncertain Income

This one won't apply so much to you if you're a teenager living with your parents who provide you with food and a roof over your head. However, we'll take a look at it anyway, so that you can get a comprehensive idea of all the risks involved.

Starting your own business can be financially uncertain, especially in the beginning. You might not have a regular paycheck for a while, and your income can be unpredictable. For example, if you launch an online store selling handmade crafts, some months may be better than others when it comes to sales. This is why entrepreneurs need to be able to budget.

Responsibility Overload

When you're the boss, you're responsible for every aspect of your business. From the big decisions like what products to offer or how to market them, to the small details like managing inventory and customer service. It can be overwhelming, especially if you still have school work and a social and family life.

No Safety Net

This one is also for the older entrepreneurs whose parents aren't providing for their basic needs, but it's good to know about it all the same. When you're an entrepreneur, there's no safety net like a traditional job. You're on your own, and it's very possible that you might fail. You need grit and resilience to keep going, even when things get tough and it looks like the business might not work out. If you face challenges, you have to be able to persevere and adapt.

Work-Life Balance

The line between work and personal life can blur when you're an entrepreneur. You might find yourself working around the clock to keep your business afloat. Balancing school, personal life, and your business can be a challenge. For example, if you're a young tech enthusiast who is creating a mobile app you could find it difficult to keep up with managing your school assignments and social activities while also developing and marketing your app.

Risk and Stress

The risks of entrepreneurship can be stressful. You're putting your time, money, and effort on the line, and that can be nerve-wracking. For example, you could start a small lawn care business and take risks by investing in equipment and marketing. If you have a period with few customers, it can be stressful as you've invested your savings into the venture.

THE TRAITS OF A SUCCESSFUL ENTREPRENEUR

There are certain character traits that can help you be successful as an entrepreneur.

Strong Leadership Qualities

Strong leadership qualities will count in your favor, as you need to inspire and guide your business team to be successful. For example, think about starting a school club. You have to have a vision for the club and need to be able to motivate your peers to work together to make it a success.

Self-Motivated

As an entrepreneur, you need to be incredibly self-motivated. You need to have an inner drive to push yourself even when you're faced with challenges. For example, you might decide to start an online art store. Once you start, you need to motivate yourself to create new artwork, manage the online store, and promote your work without anyone supervising them. You basically need to keep going after you start, otherwise, your store won't be a success.

Strong Sense of Ethics and Integrity

Entrepreneurs make decisions that are not only good for their business but also for society. For example, if you decide to start a small clothing brand you should ensure your products are ethically produced, with fair labor practices and sustainable materials.

Willingness to Fail

You're able to accept failure as part of your entrepreneurial journey. For example, you might decide to start a YouTube channel. Your early videos might not get many views, but if you keep learning and improving and understanding that each video—even if it doesn't go viral—is a learning opportunity, you will eventually achieve success.

Serial Innovators

Successful entrepreneurs can keep coming up with new ideas and solutions to problems. For example, if you're passionate about environmental issues and you create a series of eco-friendly products, such as reusable shopping bags, upcycled fashion, and organic soaps.

Know What You Don't Know

Entrepreneurs recognize that they can't be experts in everything, and they try to learn from others. For example, if you have a tech startup idea and you reach out to mentors or join coding classes to gain the knowledge and skills you need.

Competitive Spirit

A competitive spirit will encourage you to continually improve as an entrepreneur. Imagine a teenager who enjoys creating digital art. They see others in online art communities gaining recognition and strive to enhance their skills and create even more impressive artwork.

Understand the Value of a Strong Peer Network

Successful entrepreneurs understand that they can't do everything alone. You will need to build a strong network of peers and mentors. For example, if you have a passion for photography you could join photography clubs or forums to connect with like-minded individuals and gain more knowledge.

FINDING YOUR PASSION AND IDENTIFYING BUSINESS OPPORTUNITIES

Before you can start your business, you need to discover your passion and identify business opportunities. Here's how you can go about doing this.

When you set out to start your business, you should think about what you already enjoy doing. Think back to times when you were super excited about what you were doing. Those moments hold the secret to your passions. What is particularly exciting is that your passion can be the foundation for a successful business. You could end up making money from your hobbies. For example, if you enjoy making healthy food and snacks, you can think of finding a way of marketing and distributing them to others.

Also, surround yourself with people who love what they do and talk to them about their experiences. They'll inspire you.

You should also look at tying the things you enjoy doing together. Try to find common threads among your interests. For example, if you enjoy painting, drawing, and creating art, and you're into technology and programming, you can look at offering both a graphic and web design service.

You should evaluate which of your interests has the potential to solve a problem or meet a need in the market. There needs to be a demand for what you want to do, not all of your hobbies would be profitable and should be monetized. It will save you time and money if you first do research about which of your hobbies would be worth turning into a business.

Fear of failure is something you'll need to overcome before you can make headway with your business. A business will always involve financial concerns and uncertainty. Acknowledge your fears, break them down into more manageable steps, and concentrate on overcoming them.

Begin small when you start out. First research your field, and then find mentors and online resources that can give you guidance. You'll probably have to take some risks, but these don't necessarily have to be scary. For example, enroll in classes that give you the skills you need.

Finally, your journey to finding your passion and dream job is all about blending what you love with what you do for a living. It can be an exciting phase of self-discovery and growth.

Starting Your Business

It's exciting and rewarding to start your own business. Before you can get started, you need to brainstorm and come up with a plan.

Brainstorming Ideas

Begin by brainstorming business ideas that align with your interests, skills, and passions. Consider what you're good at and what you love to do. It could be anything from starting a small online store to offering tutoring services in the school subjects that you're good at.

Conducting Research

You need to research your business idea thoroughly. Study your target audience, market trends, and competitors. For example, if you plan to sell handmade health food, explore the demand for your products, what the ingredients will cost you, and where you will be able to buy them.

Put Your Plan Into Action

Once you've done your planning and research, it's time to put your plan into action. Find out what resources you need and create a business plan. You also need to figure out how you will fund your business. This could be through your savings, family support, or even crowdfunding. If you're running an online business, set up a user-friendly website or online store.

Taking Your Business to the Next Level

As your business grows, look for opportunities to take it to the next level. You should always be working on developing and growing your business. This could mean expanding your product or service offerings, increasing your customer base, and looking at new ways of marketing it. Stay open to learning from your experiences and adapt your business according to what you've learned.

TEENAGERS WHO STARTED SUCCESSFUL BUSINESSES

Let's walk along with three teenagers who managed to start successful businesses.

Shubham Banerjee

The remarkable story of Shubham Banerjee's began when he was 13 years old and he introduced his own creation, a Braille printer, at his school's 7th-grade science fair. The typical cost of Braille printers was well over £1,500, but Banerjee's innovative design came in at just £250. When his idea became more popular, he decided to share the design and software freely with others.

Following his initial success, Banerjee went on to establish a company aimed at manufacturing Braigo v2.0, with the support of an investment from Intel. He got well-deserved recognition for his brilliant idea, and he's using this to advance his vision further.

Juliette Brindak

Juliette Brindak entered the online world as a teenager with a unique vision. At the age of 16, she created a social networking site specifically for tween and teenage girls. She got her idea from the belief that girls in this age group needed a safe and exclusive space where they could connect. Brindak also personalized the platform by adding cartoon characters she had drawn as a child.

The website's mission was clear: to offer girls a secure place to discuss their experiences, look for advice, and just have fun. With the support of her family, Brindak brought her vision to life. By 2012, the website was enjoying a remarkable success, with approximately 10 million monthly visitors and a value of about $15 million.

Benjamin Stern

At the young age of 14, Benjamin Stern got an idea while he was watching a documentary that shed light on the vast amount of unrecycled plastic waste, particularly in the form of shampoo bottles found in bathrooms. He decided to create single-use shampoo pods enclosed in biodegradable, plant-based packaging. He started fundraising to bring his idea to life. With the support of his family, he launched his company by the time he turned 16.

Stern's Nohbo shampoo balls remain solid until they come into contact with water, eliminating the risk of leaks in your bag. Environmental consciousness is at the core of this product, as Stern proudly highlights that the balls are plant-based and animal cruelty-free. They're also free from parabens and sulfates.

In the next chapter of the book, we're going to look at how you can overcome villains and bounce back from adversity in your life.

BUSINESS OPPORTUNITIES

You should consider the following business types that also align with wellness and well-being. The following businesses shouldn't be too hard to manage along with your schoolwork.

You can offer online coaching or tutoring services in subjects you excel in, whether it's academics, sports, or music. This can mostly be done in the comfort of your own home unless it's very specific sports coaching.

If you're passionate about fitness and nutrition, you can become a fitness coach and offer workout plans, meal guidance, or online classes. In this way, you're also helping others by living healthier lifestyles.

Creating a blog or a YouTube channel about health, wellness, or personal development can be an excellent way to share knowledge, connect with your audience, and eventually monetize through ads or affiliate marketing. This is something that's easy to do while you're still at school, as you can just log on to your business once you've taken care of your other obligations.

You could even set up an online store that sells health and wellness products, focusing on drop shipping to minimize inventory costs. E-commerce can be done through platforms like Shopify or Etsy.

If you have coding skills, you can also use them to create health or fitness-related mobile apps. This can be done as a solo project or in collaboration with others.

Offering social media management services to small businesses, particularly those in the health and wellness sector, for example, a chiropractor's office could also be a viable business.

Teens with crafting skills can create and sell handmade wellness products like natural soaps, candles, or jewelry online or at local markets.

Writing articles or creating graphics for health and wellness blogs, magazines, or social media accounts can be a source of income for teens with writing or design skills. Even if these online jobs don't pay that well to begin with, it's also a way of building skills for your future career, and it could help you decide which field you want to study or undergo further training.

If you love animals, you can offer pet sitting, dog walking, or pet grooming services, which can be not only a profitable venture but can help you stay active.

If you have good organizational skills and a passion for wellness, you can plan and organize wellness events, retreats, or fitness workshops in your area.

When you're starting out, focus on businesses that match your skills, interests, and resources. Consider the legal requirements, such as permits or parental consent. Regardless of the chosen business, maintaining a balance between entrepreneurship and personal well-being is essential to their long-term success and happiness.

WORKSHEET: IDENTIFYING BUSINESS OPPORTUNITIES

This worksheet will help you identify potential business opportunities within the health and wellness industry. It guides you through a series of questions and exercises to find areas where you can make a positive impact.

Work on these questions in a quiet and comfortable place. Be honest and creative in the way you answer them.

Self-Reflection

- What are your personal interests and passions when it comes to health and wellness?

_____

_____

_____

- List your skills, such as research, cooking, fitness, or communication.

_____

_____

_____

- Think about health issues or challenges you or your family have faced. Are there any areas where you'd like to see improvements or solutions?

_____

_____

_____

Market Research

- Research the current health and wellness trends. What products or services are becoming more popular?

_____

- Investigate local or global health challenges and gaps in the market. Are there unmet needs or underserved communities?

_____

_____

_____

- Explore your community or school for health-related issues or concerns. Speak with peers, teachers, or parents to gather insights. Summarize your findings below.

_____

_____

_____

Identify Your Target Audience

- Define the specific group of people you want to help or serve (e.g., athletes, children, people with specific conditions).

_____

_____

_____

- Consider their demographics, interests, and needs. What are the problems they face regarding health and wellness?

_____

_____

_____

Brainstorming

- Generate a list of health and wellness business ideas based on your interests, skills, and market research. Be creative and don't limit yourself.

_____

_____

- Think about products, services, or solutions that address the needs of your target audience.

_____

_____

_____

Evaluating Ideas

- Review your list of ideas and choose one that you think will work for your target audience.

_____

_____

_____

- How feasible is your chosen idea? Is it something you can realistically pursue with the resources you have available?

_____

_____

_____

- Consider the potential impact and benefits your idea could bring to your target audience and the community.

Unique Selling Proposition (USP)

- Define what makes your idea unique or better than existing solutions in the market.

- How does your idea address the needs of your target audience in a way that sets you apart from the competition?

Prototype or Concept

- Create a rough sketch or concept of your product or service. This could be a simple drawing, outline, or description.

- Think about how your idea will work, what it will look like, and how it will benefit your target audience.

- If it's a service, outline the steps and processes involved.

Feedback and Refinement

- Share your concept with a trusted friend, family member, or mentor and gather feedback. Record the feedback below.

_____

_____

_____

- Use this feedback to refine your idea and make necessary adjustments. List those adjustments in the space provided.

_____

_____

_____

Next Steps and Action Plan

- Outline the steps you need to take to move forward with your healthypreneur idea.

_____

_____

_____

- Consider aspects like research, development, funding, and marketing.

_____

_____

_____

Ongoing Exploration

Commit to exploring new trends, attending relevant events, and continuously researching the health and wellness field.

Keep a notebook or digital journal to write down the ideas and insights that may lead to future opportunities.

Final Thoughts

- Reflect on how this exercise has helped you identify a healthypreneur opportunity.

_____

_____

_____

- Set a goal or timeframe for when you plan to take the first step toward making your idea a reality.

_____

_____

_____

The health and wellness industry is large and there are many different opportunities that you can explore.

KEY TAKEAWAYS

- Entrepreneurship is the ultimate adventure in creativity, innovation, and problem-solving.
- As a teenager, you can identify problems, find solutions, and take the initiative to make things happen.
- Being an entrepreneur is about being a problem solver, thinking outside the box, and dreaming big.
- It's a responsibility that involves taking charge of making your dreams a reality, often without relying on adults for answers.
- Entrepreneurship provides practical life experience and the opportunity to learn by doing.
- Entrepreneurship offers you freedom and independence in setting schedules and work locations.

- It allows you to pursue your passion in life.
- One of the disadvantages of entrepreneurship is an uncertain income, especially in the initial stages of the business. You also don't have job security.
- As an entrepreneur, you need to be willing to accept failure as part of the journey.
- You need to have the ability to come up with new ideas and solutions, and also be willing to learn from others.
- You need the desire to continually improve.
- Offer online coaching or tutoring services in subjects you excel in, from academics to sports or music.
- Become a fitness coach and provide workout plans, meal guidance, or online classes to promote healthier lifestyles.
- Create a blog or YouTube channel about health, wellness, or personal development, which can be managed around school commitments.
- Set up an online store selling health and wellness products, focusing on drop shipping to minimize inventory costs.
- Use coding skills to create health or fitness-related mobile apps, either as a solo project or in collaboration with others.
- Offer social media management services to small businesses, especially those in the health and wellness sector.

- Craft and sell handmade wellness items like natural soaps, candles, or jewelry online or at local markets.
- Write articles or create graphics for health and wellness publications, building skills for your future career.
- Offer pet sitting, dog walking, or pet grooming services for pet lovers while staying active.
- Plan wellness events, retreats, or fitness workshops in your area, utilizing organizational skills and passion for wellness.

STRATEGY 5

OVERCOMING VILLAINS AND BOUNCING BACK

Winners are not afraid of losing. But losers are. Failure is part of the process of success. People who avoid failure also avoid success.

— ROBERT KIYOSAKI

Mia was a teenager with big dreams, but she didn't realize she would face challenges that would test her resilience.

She has always been passionate about art, especially painting. Her dream was to become a well-known artist who would produce work that would touch people's hearts. However, in her sophomore year, she was diagnosed with a medical condition that affected her vision. She felt that the universe had conspired to rob her of her greatest passion.

The diagnosis was devastating, and she felt as if her world was falling apart. The thought of not being able to see the beautiful colors of her own creations was almost unbearable.

But Mia didn't give in to her despair and decided to fight back. She learned about techniques that worked well for other artists with visual impairment. She also met some of these artists and asked them for their guidance. Mia knew that the only thing she could do was to fight against this adversity that was threatening to kill her dreams.

Mia discovered the world of tactile art and learned how to use her other senses to create. The touch of the canvas, the smell of the paints, and the rhythm of her heartbeats guided her strokes. She learned how to use her hands to feel the texture of her artwork.

Her resilience and grit also inspired others, and she was able to determine her path.

Mia became a well-known name in the world of art. Her unique approach to painting, born out of adversity, touched people's hearts. She was invited to art exhibitions and interviewed by magazines. Her story was a testament to the superpower of resilience.

Mia's story demonstrates the superpowers of resilience and grit. We all have the superpowers of resilience and grit, even though they might not have been fully developed yet as teenagers. Imagine resilience as the shield that helps you stand strong against the villains in your life story—the setbacks, challenges, and adversities that make you feel as if you're facing an insurmountable foe.

WHAT IS RESILIENCE AND GRIT?

Life can be a roller-coaster with unexpected dips and turns. It's not always smooth sailing. Resilience is what helps you stay strong and positive even when you have to deal with setbacks and disappointments.

Most of us have learned to ride bikes as children. You've probably wobbled and fallen off a few times. Resilience is what keeps you going and getting back on that bike, even when you've got a scraped knee, and then trying until you can pedal without a hitch. Resilience is that inner voice that tells you that you can do something.

Resilience isn't about avoiding problems; it's about facing them head-on. You're like you're own superhero; ready to tackle the challenges you come across in your life. When you fail a test, have a disagreement with a friend, or face any tough situation, resilience helps you handle all setbacks with a positive attitude.

Resilience can be practiced and strengthened over time. Every time you overcome a challenge, your resilience grows a little stronger. It's a superpower that helps you keep going, learn from your experiences, and come out even more powerful and confident.

So what is grit and perseverance? Grit is like the engine that drives you toward your long-term goals. It's that inner fire that keeps you going, no matter how tough the journey becomes. It's the determination and passion that fuel your dreams.

Grit is all about hanging in there, even when the going gets tough. It's not giving up on your dreams when faced with challenges. When you have grit you keep moving forward, even if the path is steep.

Grit is fueled by your deep love and enthusiasm for what you're pursuing. It's that burning desire to reach your goals. Think of it as a flame that keeps you warm even during cold times.

Grit is the long-term effort you put into something, that you can compare to a marathon. You're prepared to put in the same amount of hard work day after day. Just like a long-distance runner, you keep going, step by step, until you finally get to where you want to be.

No matter how many times you stumble or face setbacks, grit encourages you to get back up and try again.

Strengthening Your Resilience

There are practical ways in which you can develop your resilience and become more confident.

- You need to develop self-awareness and this involves understanding your emotional responses to stress. Take a moment to recognize how you react when things get tough. Awareness is the first step to building resilience.
- Try to reframe your thoughts when you're stressed, instead of reacting in impulsive ways. You should approach situations with a balanced perspective and rethink your initial reaction to things, especially if it's overly negative.

- Don't get stuck in all-or-nothing thinking when facing problems. Focus on pinpointing the specific problem instead of generalizing and simply saying "Things just always go wrong."
- Keep track of your successes, even the small ones, and celebrate them. Maintaining a success journal can boost your motivation and positive emotions such as pride.
- Spread positivity wherever you go. Even simple gestures such as thanking someone when they do something for you can improve your relationship. Find a positive routine in your life, like sharing daily highlights with loved ones.
- Strengthen your social networks and share your connections with others. You should do your best to figure out what you have in common with your colleagues, friends, and family, as this will help you build deeper connections with them.
- It's part of being human to feel regret and make mistakes. Don't worry too much about them, learn and move on from them instead. Share your missteps with loved ones, laugh about them, and decide how you can do better next time.

COPING WITH FAILURE

Setbacks are like the plot twists in the adventure of healthypreneurship, and they're as inevitable as rainy days during the winter. They're the villains in your story or the hurdles in your race. They show up when you least expect them, and they can be daunting.

Failure is simply part of the game of entrepreneurship. It's almost like the "Game Over" screen in your favorite video game. When you stumble or fall, it's simply time to get up and try again. After all, the point of failure is to turn it into your stepping stone for long-term success.

So how can you, as a teenage entrepreneur, cope with your failure and even turn it into success?

Change your perspective by not seeing failure as the end of your road but rather simply as a setback. Analyzing your failure can help you do this. What went wrong? Which factors led to the setback? Did you miscalculate or make poor decisions? If you understand the causes, you can avoid similar problems in the future.

How Emma Managed to Overcome Her Business Challenges

Emma launched her custom-made jewelry store at the age of 16.

Emma wanted to craft unique, handcrafted jewelry that could tell a story. She spent hours designing and creating each piece, and she hoped her customers would like it.

Emma faced the same challenges and obstacles as any startup. At first, her business received only a few orders. Despite her belief that her product was unique, the market was saturated with similar products, and it was difficult to stand out. She was working hard, but felt she wasn't gaining anything from it.

Then she experienced her first major setback. A larger jewelry company released a similar product, and they could afford to market it aggressively. Her sales fell further, and Emma felt as if her dream was slipping away from her.

However, she wasn't one to give up that easily. Instead, she saw this setback as an opportunity for growth, and took the opportunity to figure out her business model, and how she could bounce back stronger. She sought advice from other entrepreneurs who shared their insights and experiences with her.

Emma realized that her business needed a unique selling point. She revamped her designs to focus on eco-friendly, sustainable materials, appealing to a niche market of environmentally conscious consumers. She also used social media to show how committed she is to sustainability and to spread the word about her creations.

Emma relaunched her business with renewed passion. She used recycled materials for her jewelry and highlighted the importance of ethical and environmentally friendly practices. Emma's brand now stood for making a positive impact on the planet.

The response was more than she had been hoping for. People who shared Emma's values flocked to her online store. They admired her dedication to sustainability and her beautifully handcrafted jewelry. Her unique selling point set her apart from the competition and gained her a loyal customer base.

Emma's passion for sustainability was clear in her creations, and her customers appreciated the craftsmanship behind each piece.

Emma realized that her failures had taught her the resilience, adaptability, and determination she needed to be successful in the competitive business world.

HOW TO BECOME A HIGH ACHIEVER

Becoming a high achiever in life is a journey that can start in your teenage years. This is the time you can get ahead by setting big goals, working hard, and developing important life skills.

As a teenager, you're still exploring your passions and interests, which will help you find your purpose. For example, if you're passionate about the environment, you can engage in local conservation projects or start an eco club at school. Your greater purpose could be to make a positive impact on the planet.

Be enthusiastic about pursuing your dreams. Let's say you're passionate about music and your goal is to learn a musical instrument and play in a band. Being passionate means practicing your instrument not because you have to but because you love it. It's about jamming with friends, writing songs, and dedicating time to your musical dream.

It's important to embrace lifelong learning while you're still young. For example, if you want to become a skilled basketball player, practice is essential. It's like shooting hoops for hours, working on your dribbling skills, and participating in pick-up games. You have to understand that making mistakes is part of practice, and it's how you grow.

You might be scared of trying new things, like joining a debate club or auditioning for a school play. Having the courage to try means stepping out of your comfort zone, even if you're nervous. When you audition for the school play you'll realize that the stage isn't as scary as you thought.

Never give up on what you want, even when the going is tough. Imagine you're working on a challenging science project, and you're tempted to quit. Perseverance means pushing through the tough parts, looking for help when you need it, and completing the project. You understand it's okay to struggle, but that doesn't mean you should give up.

You need to develop the ability to bounce back from setbacks. In your teenage years, you might face setbacks like not making the sports team you wanted. Resiliency is about bouncing back, trying again next year, and using the experience to improve. It's understanding that failures are opportunities to grow stronger.

For teenagers, becoming a high achiever means embracing your passions, having the courage to try new things, and understanding that practice and perseverance are the keys to success. If you adopt these steps you can set a strong foundation for your future achievements.

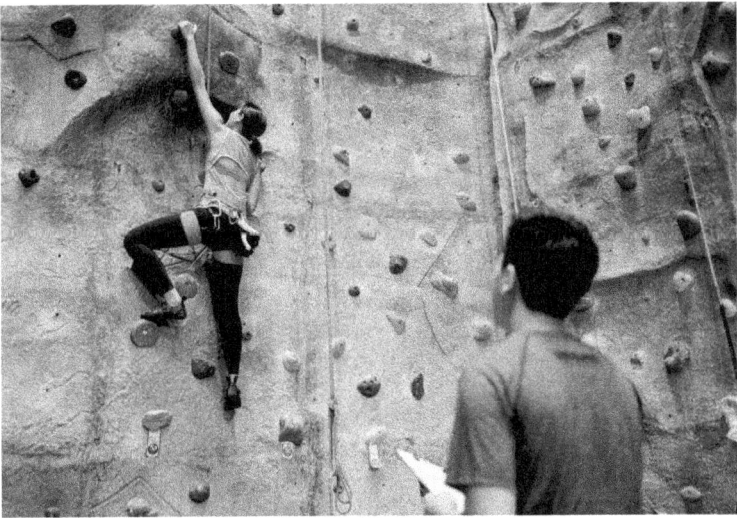

RESILIENCE BUILDING ACTIVITIES AND STRATEGIES

The following activities can help you develop resilience.

Mindfulness Meditation

Mindfulness meditation can help you stay grounded and reduce stress. Regular practice can help you become better at emotional regulation, and also more focused.

Goal Setting

Set achievable goals. This can help you stay motivated when you have to deal with obstacles.

Physical Activity

Social Support

Building strong relationships with friends, family, or mentors can provide a support system during tough times.

Problem-Solving Skills

Develop effective problem-solving strategies. This includes breaking challenges into smaller steps and finding solutions.

Gratitude Practice

Regularly reflecting on the things you're grateful for can improve your outlook on life and help you focus on the positive.

Resilience Stories

Read motivational stories of resilience from other teenagers.

Role-Playing Scenarios

Engage in role-play activities where you can practice handling difficult situations such as conflicts or peer pressure.

Stress Management Techniques

Practice stress reduction techniques like deep breathing, progressive muscle relaxation, or time management.

Volunteer Work

Volunteering can give you a sense of purpose and a broader perspective on life's challenges.

Creative Outlets

Express yourself creatively through art, music, or writing.

Emotional Regulation Skills

Identify and manage your emotions, such as anger, frustration, or anxiety.

Positive Role Models

Look up to positive role models who have demonstrated resilience in their lives.

Coping Strategies Toolbox

Create a toolbox of coping strategies. When you encounter adversity, you can choose from this toolkit.

Support Groups

If you're facing specific challenges like loss or addiction, consider support groups that provide a safe space to connect with others who understand.

Encourage Independence

Take responsibility for your decisions and learn from both your successes and mistakes.

Healthy Lifestyle Choices

Get enough sleep, maintain a balanced diet, and limit substance use.

Seek Professional Help

If you're struggling with a severe mental health issue, you should seek help from mental health professionals.

SHOULD YOU CONTINUE YOUR STUDIES OR JUST FOCUS ON YOUR BUSINESS?

If you're almost at the end of your school career, you're probably faced with the choice of continuing your studies or just focusing on your business. So, how do you decide? We'll look at some points that can help you make up your mind.

Advantages of Continuing Studies

There are various advantages to further studies, even though you might feel that it's going to take up a lot of your time.

Higher education can broaden your skill set, which will be valuable for your business. You might learn about finance, marketing, and management, among other skills.

College or university provides a unique environment for building connections. You can meet potential partners, mentors, or even customers. However, make sure that you always stay true to your authentic self, and connect to people whose values are the same as yours.

Education can serve as a safety net. If your entrepreneurial venture faces challenges, having a degree to fall back on can be reassuring. Many entrepreneurs have faced several business failures and have only really achieved success after several attempts. A degree at least gives you the option of finding a job while you're working on your future business ideas.

Some institutions offer programs and resources specifically designed for budding entrepreneurs. These can help you refine your business skills.

Advantages of Focusing on Your Business

On the other hand, your own business provides hands-on experience that no classroom can replicate. You'll encounter real challenges and learn to adapt. You'll often find you learn better from practical experience than from the theory you find in books.

A business often demands a significant amount of time and energy. By focusing exclusively on it, you can accelerate its growth and development. It can be extremely challenging to split your energy between several endeavors.

Studying at a college or university can be expensive. If you're managing a business, you might prefer to reinvest the money you earn into your business. However, if you're already running a profitable business before you leave school, this may enable you to study without taking expensive study loans.

Factors to Consider

There are certain factors you need to consider when it comes to studying or focusing on your business.

Consider the stage of your business. If it's in the early stages and needs significant attention, it might be the better option to prioritize it for the moment.

Assess your financial situation and funding requirements for both your business and education. This will also affect your decision.

Think about your long-term goals. What do you want to achieve with your business, and how does education fit into that vision? While you don't need the qualification at the moment, might you possibly need it in the future?

It's possible to balance education and entrepreneurship, but it can be challenging. If you're up for the challenge, part-time or online courses might be a compromise. Over the past few years, many universities have made online options available, which gives you the option of working and studying at the same time.

Ultimately, your decision should align with your aspirations and the specific circumstances of your business. It's important to weigh the pros and cons carefully and ask mentors who can help you make an informed choice for advice.

WORKSHEET: BUILDING RESILIENCE

This worksheet will help you build resilience, which is the ability to bounce back from adversity, grow stronger through challenges, and adapt to life's ups and downs. Do the following exercises in your journal.

Self-Reflection

- Think about challenging situations you've faced in the past. It could be an academic setback, a fight with a friend, or any other challenge. Write a brief description of the situation, how you felt, and how you handled it.

_____

_____

_____

Positive Thinking

- Think about the situation you described in the previous step. Identify any negative or self-critical thoughts that emerged during that time. Write them down.

_____

_____

_____

- Now, challenge your negative thoughts with positive and more realistic perspectives.

_____

_____

_____

Understanding Emotions

- Reflect on how you felt during the challenging situation. Did you feel angry, sad, or frustrated?

_____

_____

_____

- What physical sensations did you feel, such as your heart beating fast?

_____

_____

_____

- Acknowledge that it's natural to feel these emotions and that it's a normal stress response. You can write an affirmation to help you if you'd like.

_____

_____

_____

Building a Support System

- List three people you can turn to for support when facing challenges. These could be friends, family members, teachers, or mentors.

_____

_____

_____

- Reflect on how you can communicate your feelings to these people and ask for their guidance or encouragement.

_____

_____

_____

Problem-Solving Skills

- Think about the challenging situation you've faced. What were some practical steps you could have taken to address it or reduce the impact of your problem?

_____

_____

_____

- Write down at least three potential solutions or strategies for handling similar challenges in the future.

_____

_____

_____

Resilience Stories

Find a story of resilience from someone you admire or even a historical figure who faced significant adversity. Summarize their story and the key lessons you can draw from it.

_____

_____

_____

Coping Strategies

- List three healthy coping strategies that work for you when dealing with stress and adversity (e.g., deep breathing, mindfulness, physical activity).

_____

_____

_____

- Describe how you make these strategies part of your daily life.

_____

_____

Setting Goals

- Think about a personal goal you'd like to achieve in the future. It could be related to academics, hobbies, or personal growth. Write down the specific goal, a timeline, and a plan for achieving it.

_____

_____

_____

Self-Compassion

Reflect on the idea that it's okay to make mistakes and face challenges. Nobody is perfect. Write a compassionate message to yourself, encouraging yourself to be kind to yourself.

_____

_____

_____

Action Plan

Based on the insights and strategies you've explored in this worksheet, create an action plan for building your resilience.

Outline specific steps you will take to strengthen your ability to bounce back from challenges.

_____

_____

_____

_____

_____

_____

Final Thoughts

Think about how completing this worksheet has helped you understand and build your resilience.

_____

_____

_____

KEY TAKEAWAYS

- Resilience is the ability to stay positive and strong in the face of setbacks and disappointments.
- Resilience can help you deal with life's challenges.

- Resilience can be developed and strengthened over time.
- Grit and perseverance are the determination and passion that fuel long-term goals.
- Grit can be compared to an engine that drives you toward your aspirations.
- Grit can help you maintain determination when you have to deal with challenges.
- The first step in building resilience is the development of self-awareness and balanced perspectives.
- Practical strategies for building resilience are reframing your thoughts, avoiding all-or-nothing thinking, celebrating successes, and fostering positivity.
- You will also build your resilience if you strengthen your social networks and learn from your mistakes.
- You can cope with failure by changing your perspective, analyzing the causes, and using setbacks as opportunities for growth.
- Emma's story of overcoming challenges in her jewelry business is an example of using failure as a stepping stone to success.
- You can become a high achiever in life by focusing on your passion, practice, courage, perseverance, and resilience.
- If you struggle with severe mental health issues, you should seek professional help.

STRATEGY 6

SOCIAL MEDIA: YOUR BUSINESS'S SECRET SUPERPOWER

In today's digital age, social media is not an option for businesses; it's a necessity for survival.

— MICROSOFT'S CEO SATYA NADELLA

Being able to use the power of social media can be a game changer for your business in the digital age. If you use the right strategies, you can create a strong brand, and reach a global audience.

We'll look at the various ways you can use platforms like Facebook, Instagram, Twitter, LinkedIn, and others to enhance your brand and communicate with your audience. Before you jump in and start creating your social media platforms, you need to take the first steps by creating a brand identity for your business.

CREATING A BRAND IDENTITY

Deciding on an identity for your brand before creating your social media pages is extremely important because it will help you create a consistent presence online. Your brand identity includes your brand's personality, values, mission, and visual elements.

Here's how you can develop your brand identity:

Define Your Brand's Mission and Values

Start by clarifying the purpose of your brand. What problem does your business solve? What values do you stand for?

Determine the core values and principles that guide your brand. These will be the basis for the content you share on social media.

Identify Your Target Audience

Understand who your ideal customers are. What are their demographics, interests, and pain points? If you know your audience well, you can tailor your social media to connect with them.

Create Your Brand Voice

Decide on the tone and personality of your brand. Are you friendly, professional, casual, or authoritative? Your target audience should be able to relate to your brand voice.

Choose Visual Elements

Decide on the visual elements that will represent your brand. This includes your logo, color palette, typography, and any other design elements. Your visuals need to be consistent across all your platforms, as it will make it easier to recognize your brand.

Craft Your Unique Selling Proposition (USP)

What sets your brand apart from your competition? You should use this unique selling point in your social media messaging.

Develop a Brand Story

This can be a powerful way to connect with your audience. Share the story of how your brand was founded, your journey, and the impact you aim to make in your industry.

Create a Brand Style Guide

Develop a brand style guide that explains all the elements of your brand identity. This guide will make sure your social media content is consistent.

Competitive Analysis

Study your competitors and similar brands in your industry. Understand what strategies have worked for them and what you could do differently to make yourself stand out.

Test and Refine

Launch your social media profiles with your chosen brand identity, but be prepared to amend it as you get feedback from your audience and gain more insight.

A SOCIAL MEDIA STRATEGY FOR YOUR BUSINESS

You probably have personal accounts on different social media platforms that you use to communicate with your friends. It can be fun to share posts and photos of good times you've had with your friends.

Did you know that you can also use social media to grow your business? If you've used different platforms in your personal capacity, you already have a good start.

So, let's take a look at why your business needs a social media strategy.

Social media platforms have billions of active users worldwide. If you have a well-crafted strategy you can make your products more visible to your customers, and also reach more potential new customers.

What does a good social media strategy look like?

It will outline your business's objectives, target audience, and how you will approach your content, and involve creating a posting schedule. You should also be able to measure the success of your marketing campaigns by using tools such as Google Analytics. A good social media plan is a roadmap that guides your social media efforts and makes sure that they not only align with your business goals but that they also have a positive effect on your audience.

Information to Include in Your Strategy

Your well-crafted plan should include the following information:

- Define specific, measurable, and time-bound objectives. Do you want to increase awareness of your brand, drive traffic to your website, boost sales of your products and services, or improve customer engagement?

- You need to know your target audience, and who your ideal customers are. Understand their demographics, interests, and behaviors. This information will help you create the best content to make an impact on them.
- Choose the social media platforms that align with your business goals, but that are also used by your target audience. Each platform has unique characteristics and user demographics. For example, if you want to reach mostly young people, you can look at marketing on TikTok.
- Does your business have competitors? Study their social media and try to figure out what they're doing well. What can you do better? Once you have an understanding of this, you can amend your social media strategy.
- You'll also need to think about the type of content you'll create and share. This can include blog posts, videos, infographics, user-generated content, and more. Create a content calendar to plan your posts in advance.
- Establish a consistent posting schedule based on the platforms you're using. Different platforms have optimal posting times, so you need to do some research and then schedule your posts according to this.
- Figure out how you're going to interact with your audience on social media. Respond to comments and messages, and take part in conversations

relevant to your industry. How will you manage negative comments and deal with social media trolls?

- If you have some money for paid advertising, you can look at platforms like Facebook Ads or Instagram Ads.
- If you know someone who is an influencer on social media and has lots of followers, they can also help you promote your products and services. A social media influencer is a person with credibility and a dedicated following in a specific niche or industry on social media platforms. They use their online presence to impact the opinions, behaviors, or decisions of their audience through content, endorsements, and recommendations.
- Research and use relevant hashtags to increase the visibility of your content. A hashtag is a keyword or phrase preceded by the "#" symbol (e.g., #Travel, #Foodie). It is used on social media platforms to categorize and group content that's about a specific topic or theme. Hashtags make it easier for users to discover and interact with posts, discussions, and trends.
- Define your brand's voice and tone on social media. Are you friendly and casual or formal and informative? You have to be consistent across all the platforms you use.
- Develop a crisis management plan for handling negative comments, reviews, or other PR issues.

The reality is that you may have to deal with cyberbullying and trolls. You may even have to deal with "concern trolls" who don't seem so harmful at first. A concern troll pretends to be genuinely concerned about a specific topic, issue, or group, but they really want to provoke or criticize. Concern trolls often engage in online discussions or forums under the guise of offering helpful advice or expressing worry, but their underlying motive is to turn people against each other. They challenge opinions or undermine the credibility of those they're engaging with.

- You need to define key performance indicators (KPIs) to track the success of your strategy. Common metrics include engagement rate, reach, website traffic, leads generated, and sales conversion.
- Create a schedule for reviewing and reporting on your social media performance. Regular assessment can help you change and improve your strategy.
- You must make sure that your social media activities adhere to legal and regulatory guidelines relevant to your industry.
- A well-crafted social media strategy is not static. It will have to be amended as your business grows and as the social media landscape changes.

The Benefits of a Social Media Strategy

There are many benefits to having a social media strategy for your business.

Social media platforms are rich sources of data. Your strategy can involve monitoring and analyzing customer interactions, which will give you insight into market trends, preferences, and competition.

Social media is a cost-effective and fast marketing tool. You can create targeted ad campaigns to reach specific demographics, boosting the visibility of your products or services around the globe. It's no longer necessary to spend a lot of money on printed marketing material.

Consistent and meaningful interactions on social media can help you build a loyal customer base. By sharing valuable content and addressing customer needs, you can turn one-time buyers into your loyal supporters.

A social media strategy helps you respond quickly to any negative developments or crises that may affect your business. You can address issues transparently and manage your business reputation effectively.

Social media can drive traffic to your website. Sharing blog posts, product pages, or other content can send users to your website where they can learn more and make purchases. If you don't have a business website, you should consider creating one or getting someone to help you create one. We'll take a look later on in this book on how you can create a website quickly and almost effortlessly. This is also an opportunity to gain useful computer skills that can help you later on in your career. Who knows, you could even set up a side hustle as a web designer.

A strategy will help you to set goals and metrics for tracking your social media success. You can use analytics to measure the performance of your social media efforts and adjust your strategy accordingly.

Social media allows you to gather useful and almost instant feedback from customers. You can learn what they like or dislike about your products and services and make improvements. For example, customers can leave you feedback in the comments they add to your social media platforms.

BEST SOCIAL MEDIA PLATFORMS FOR TEEN ENTREPRENEURS

The platform you will use will depend on different factors. You will need to consider the type of audience you want to target, and also what your content strategy is going to be.

Here are some social media platforms that are popular with teenagers and that can also be a good fit for you as a teenage entrepreneur:

- Instagram is a visual platform that's popular with younger people. You can show your products and share behind-the-scenes content. You should also use Instagram Stories for engagement.
- TikTok is popular among teenagers and is known for its short, engaging videos. It can help you create creative content, tell your brand story, and connect with your peers.
- Snapchat is another platform preferred by teens. It's ideal for sharing time-sensitive content, offering flash deals, and connecting with younger people.
- You can also use YouTube to share video content, and use it for tutorials, vlogs, product reviews, and more. A vlog, which is short for "video blog," is a type of online content that involves the creation and sharing of videos. The video is usually diary-

like or in a documentary style and conveys personal experiences, opinions, or information to an audience.

- Twitter allows for real-time engagement and quick updates. You can share industry news and participate in trending conversations about your industry.
- Facebook is useful if you want to reach a wider audience, especially when offering products or services that appeal to a broader age range.
- If your business is focused on professional services or B2B products, LinkedIn can help you network and show others your expertise.
- If you're involved in creative niches like fashion, art, or crafts, Pinterest can help you share visual content and drive traffic to your website or online store.
- Etsy is a popular e-commerce platform if you want to sell handmade items.
- Creating a personal blog or website can be an effective way to share knowledge and expertise and promote products or services.

CREATING A PROFESSIONAL PROFILE

If you want to get attention for your business on social media, you need to know how to create a professional profile that will keep your readers coming back for more. An unprofessional profile full of mistakes and bad-quality photos will just give your business a bad name, which won't attract anyone to read more about your business.

Remember that you can also use your social media to funnel or attract customers to your website if you have one.

Creating a profile on social media is something that can take a lot of time, especially if it needs to convey a professional image.

Here are the steps to create an effective profile:

Profile Picture

Choose a clear, high-resolution image of yourself or your business logo. For personal branding, a professional headshot is ideal, while for a business, the logo is suitable.

Ensure that the image is well-lit and free from distractions.

Use the same profile picture across all social media platforms to make sure your brand is consistent.

Cover Photo

Your cover photo should complement your profile picture and reflect your brand or business theme.

It can be an image related to your products or services, a professional banner with your business name and tagline, or a visually appealing landscape relevant to your niche.

Make sure your photo has high resolution and is well composed. For example, you won't photos where you're at a party with your friends or you're enjoying a day at the beach.

Bio/About Section

Write a concise and informative bio that captures your business identity and value proposition. Use keywords relevant to your niche.

Include the necessary information such as your business name, location, website link, and a brief overview of what you offer.

If applicable, mention your unique selling points or what sets your business apart.

Use a consistent tone and style that aligns with your brand's identity.

Contact Information

Provide accurate and up-to-date contact information. This may include your email address, phone number, and physical address if you have a physical location. Use a professional email address.

Call to Action (CTA)

Some platforms allow you to include a call to action button on your profile. Use this to encourage your visitors to take specific actions, such as "Contact Us," "Learn More," or "Shop Now."

Highlights and Stories

If the platform supports highlights or stories, use these to share updates, promotions, or behind-the-scenes glimpses of your business. This can be useful if you want to show how you make certain things, e.g. craft products or baking cakes.

Credentials and Achievements

If you or your business have received awards, recognition, or certifications, consider mentioning them in your profile to build credibility.

Keywords and Hashtags

Incorporate relevant keywords and hashtags in your bio to make yourself more discoverable. For example, if you're a writer, use terms such as "creative writer" or "romance fiction."

Consistency

Make sure you use the same profile image, cover photo, and branding elements across all your platforms to help people recognize your brand.

Privacy Settings

Review and adjust privacy settings to suit your preferences. Some information may be set to public, while you might prefer to keep other details private.

Regular Updates

Always keep your profile information up to date. Update it whenever there are significant changes to your business, such as new services, products, or contact details.

Your social media profile is often the first impression potential customers will get of your business. Put some time into creating a profile that will appeal to your target audience.

PAID SOCIAL MEDIA

Paid social media is another good option for your business, especially if you're concerned about keeping trolls off your pages. However, it won't entirely keep them out, but it can help lessen their impact. If you haven't heard about trolls before (most of us have) they're people who enjoy posting offensive or disruptive content on social media. For example, if there are people who don't like you for some reason, they may post negative content about your products and services, encouraging others not to use them.

When you run paid advertising campaigns on platforms like Facebook or Instagram, you have more control over who sees your content because you can specify your target audience. Other paid social media platforms like Patreon could also be a good option.

Paid campaigns also allow you to exclude certain demographics or target a more specific group to reduce exposure to trolls.

To deal with trolls, you can also use community management strategies to monitor and moderate comments on your posts. You can hide or delete inappropriate comments, block or report users, and encourage a more positive online community.

What is Patreon?

So, let's take a look at Patreon, which is a paid platform. Patreon might be a great option for you if you run an online content creation business. It's an online platform that allows content creators to receive financial support directly from their fans or patrons. On Patreon, you can set up your account according to various membership tiers or subscription levels for your fans. In return for supporting you, your followers gain access to exclusive content and certain perks that aren't available to everyone. For example, they can be the first to view your exclusive new content.

If you're a YouTuber, podcaster, musician, artist, writer, or any other type of content creator you could use Patreon to offer different membership levels, each with its own set of rewards. These rewards can include early access to content, exclusive live streams, private community forums, or even physical merchandise like posters or T-shirts.

Patreon operates on a monthly subscription model, so your fans can support you with a recurring monthly payment. This can create a regular income to help you sustain your work and often provides a more stable and predictable source of revenue. You won't only have to rely on advertising or one-time purchases.

ACTIVITY: SOCIAL MEDIA PROFILE TEMPLATE

Here's a basic social media profile template that you can adapt for various platforms. Keep in mind that each platform has different character limits and features, so make sure your profiles meet the requirements of all the platforms.

Use the template to create your first social media profile.

Profile Picture

[Upload a clear and professional profile picture.]

[Use your logo or a high-quality headshot.]

Cover Photo

[Add a visually appealing cover photo that aligns with your brand or theme.]

Bio/About Section

Name: [Your name or business name]

Location: [Your city or region]

Website: [Your website URL]

Description: [Concise, informative description of your business.]

Contact Information

Email: [Your professional email address]

Phone: [Your contact number]

Address: [Your physical address, if applicable]

Call to Action (CTA)

[Add a CTA button if the platform allows. Choose an appropriate action, e.g., "Contact Us," "Learn More," or "Shop Now."]

Highlights/Stories

[Create and organize highlights or stories to share updates, promotions, or behind-the-scenes content.]

Credentials and Achievements

[Mention any awards, certifications, or achievements your business has earned.]

Keywords and Hashtags

[Incorporate relevant keywords and hashtags to improve discoverability.]

Privacy Settings

[Review and adjust privacy settings to control what is public or private.]

Regular Updates

[Remember to update your profile information as your business grows.]

Change this template to suit your needs on different social media platforms. It's important to keep in mind that character limits and features can be different from platform to platform.

KEY TAKEAWAYS

- Before you develop a plan for your social media, you need to start with a clear mission and core values for your brand.
- Identifying your target audience and understanding their demographics, interests, and behaviors will make it easier for you to develop social media that is relatable to them.
- Your business needs a unique brand voice and personality.
- Choose visual elements, including logos, color palettes, and typography that fit in with the vision you have for your business's brand.
- Highlight your Unique Selling Proposition (USP). Having a USP means your product or services stand out from that of your competitors. There is something distinctive that sets it apart.
- As your business grows, you will have to adapt your brand identity.
- Define specific, measurable, and time-bound objectives for your business.
- Know your target audience, their demographics, interests, and behaviors.
- Choose the right social media platforms aligned with your business goals and target audience.
- Analyze your competitors and learn from their social media strategies.

- You also need to have a strategy for the content you want to share with your followers.
- Plan your approach to interacting with your audience and handling negative comments or trolls.
- Consider using paid advertising and partnering with influencers.
- Research and use relevant hashtags to boost content visibility.
- Develop a crisis management plan to handle negative comments and PR issues.
- Make sure all your media activities are legal.
- Build a loyal customer base through interacting in a meaningful way on social media.
- Consider Instagram for visual content and Instagram Stories.
- Use TikTok for engaging short videos.
- Create video content on YouTube.
- Engage in real-time conversations on Twitter.
- Facebook can help you reach a broader audience.
- LinkedIn is a great choice if you want to market your specific expertise and you want to network with others in your field.
- Consider Etsy if your business sells handmade items.

STRATEGY 7

BUILDING YOUR EPIC BUSINESS WEBSITE

Your website is the window of your business. Keep it fresh, keep it exciting.

— JAY CONRAD LEVINSON

In today's digital age, your business needs a website, even when you're just starting out. It's your digital storefront, a 24/7 sales representative, and a powerful marketing tool that can connect you with potential customers across the globe.

It's the gateway through which potential customers learn about your business, explore your products or services, and decide if they want to buy from you.

Having a website can help you serve your customers in the most effective and efficient ways.

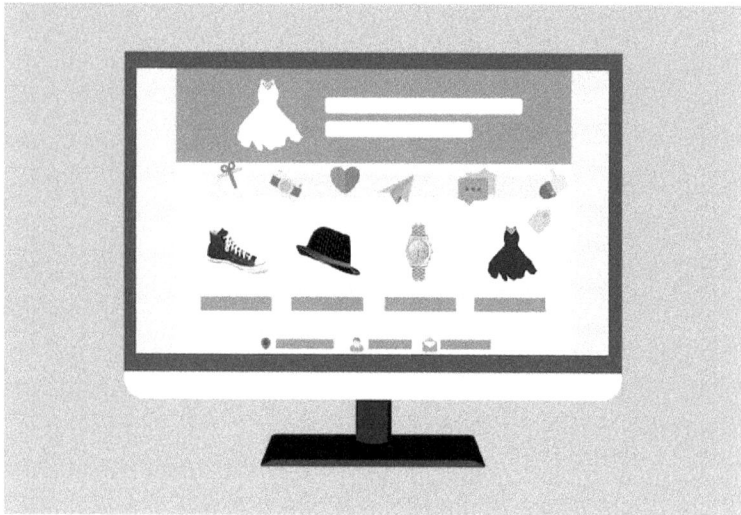

WHY YOUR BUSINESS NEEDS A WEBSITE

A well-designed and attractive website can serve as your business card and digital storefront. It gives the impression that your company is established and professional, and potential customers will be more likely to trust you and buy your services. This gives you an advantage over your competitors.

Your website is also an information hub about your business. You can share details about your products or services, contact information, pricing, and frequently asked questions. If there is a chat functionality, people can also chat with you directly on the site.

Unlike physical stores, your website is available 24/7, and customers can obtain information and buy items when they find it convenient.

Customers also find it convenient to research and shop online. Visiting your website gives them time to browse and compare products. Indecisive people who want a lot of information about products before they decide which one to buy will definitely appreciate this feature.

Websites provide a cost-effective platform for marketing and advertising your business. You can use various digital marketing strategies to reach a broad audience without having to pay a lot of money for traditional marketing.

A website also allows you to grow your customer base and reach more customers—even internationally. It also makes it easier to communicate with your customers through features like contact forms, live chat, social media integration, and email subscriptions. Customers can even communicate with you in real-time if your website has a chat functionality.

You can display your products or services with detailed descriptions, high-quality images, and even videos. This will also give your customers a better understanding of what you have to offer.

A website provides a platform for content marketing. You can create and share valuable content such as blog posts, articles, and guides to show that you're an expert in your industry.

A website also offers you the advantage of collecting data and insights about customer behavior. You can use analytics tools to track user activity, demographics, and preferences, allowing you to refine your marketing strategies.

As your business grows, your website can grow with it. You can add new pages, features, and capabilities to accommodate expanding product lines or services.

A GUIDE TO CREATING YOUR WEBSITE

It can be quite a process to create your website, but you need to start out by first deciding exactly what you want to do with it. Once you know its purpose, the rest of the process will become easier.

Define Your Website's Purpose

Decide the main purpose of your website. Is it for e-commerce, providing information, showing your portfolio, or getting clients? It will help you with the design and content if you know your website's purpose.

Choosing Your Domain Name

Select a domain name that reflects your business. Keep it simple, memorable, and relevant to your brand. Consider using your business name if possible.

You will have to purchase your domain name from a domain registrar or web hosting provider.

Choose a Website Building Platform And Hosting Provider

Choose a web hosting provider that suits your needs. Look for hosting services that offer website builders or content management systems (CMS) for easy website creation.

Popular hosting providers include Bluehost, HostGator, SiteGround, and Wix.

Site 123 is an excellent, cost-effective option for beginners. It's a user-friendly and versatile content management platform, which will make it easy for you to create and manage your website. It has an intuitive drag-and-drop interface and a wide range of beautiful templates.

Site123 makes it easy for you to create professional-looking websites without the need for extensive technical knowledge. This platform also provides hosting services, domain registration, and e-commerce capabilities, making it a one-stop solution for those looking to establish a robust online presence. It offers you a hassle-free website-building experience.

Design Your Website

Once you've picked your website builder, you can start designing your site.

Use the chosen website builder to design your site. Most platforms offer pre-designed templates that you can select and change as you want them to be.

Focus on creating a visually appealing, user-friendly, and responsive design that works well on both desktop and mobile devices. Make sure that you keep your branding consistent with your logo, colors, and style.

Basic Website Design Tips

Whether you're going to design your website yourself or get someone else to help you design it, you will find the following tips useful.

Firstly, your website needs user-friendly navigation. Make sure that your menu structure is intuitive and easy to navigate. Use clear labels and organized menus to help visitors find what they're looking for quickly. People are much more likely to come back to your website and even buy your products and services if your website is user-friendly.

Ensure your website is mobile-responsive, so it looks and functions well on different digital devices, such as smartphones and tablets.

When it comes to the visual elements of the design, branding such as your logo, color schemes, and typography need to be consistent throughout your website. This will help your brand identity become even stronger.

You can make sure your website loads fast by making sure your images are small enough, minimizing unnecessary scripts, and making sure you're using a reliable provider to host your website.

Use high-resolution images and graphics that enhance your content and support your brand. Pixelated and low-quality visuals will just create a negative impression of your business, and people might think that you're not delivering a professional product or service.

The fonts on your website need to be readable and consistent throughout your site. For example, if your font is too small, people might not be able to read it and they will just move on to the next website.

Effective use of whitespace (empty space) can also help you improve the readability of your website. Avoid cluttered layouts.

Organize content logically, with headings, subheadings, and bullet points. Use relevant categories and tags for blog posts and articles. If your website includes forms, keep them simple and easy to fill out. Minimize the required fields to encourage submissions.

Ensure your website is accessible to all users, including those with disabilities. This includes using alt text for images and providing captions for videos.

Avoid excessive pop-ups, animations, and distracting elements that may overwhelm or annoy visitors. Focus on what's essential. It's useful to have loading animations and progress bars to keep your visitors engaged while your content is loading. This will prevent them from leaving your site and becoming frustrated.

Also make sure you include social media icons and share buttons, which will make it easier to access your website through your social media accounts.

The Search Engine Optimization (SEO) Side of Web Design

Search Engine Optimization (SEO) is like the magic behind getting your website to show up on Google when you search for something. It will make your website easier to find.

SEO involves picking the right words (keywords) that people use in their searches and putting them in your website's content. You also need other websites to talk about you and say how great your site is (linking to you). The more links you have, the more Google thinks you're important, and the higher you'll show up in search results.

You also need to incorporate optimized meta tags and descriptive URLs.

An optimized meta tag is a specific type of HTML tag that is used to provide information about a web page's content to search engines and website visitors. The two most common types of meta tags are the "title" and "meta description" tags.

This is a critical meta tag that provides the title of a web page. It appears as the main clickable link in search engine results. An optimized title tag should be concise, relevant to the page's content, and contain targeted keywords to improve search engine ranking and attract user clicks.

The meta description tag provides a brief summary or description of the web page's content. An optimized meta description should be engaging and informative and include keywords to encourage users to click on the link in search results. While it doesn't directly impact search rankings, a well-crafted meta description can improve click-through rates.

```
<div class="container">
  <div class="row">
    <div class="col-md-6 col-lg-8"> <!-- _____ BEGIN NAVIGATION
      <nav id="nav" role="navigation">
        <ul>
          <li><a href="index.html">Home</a></li>
          <li><a href="home-events.html">Home Events</a></li>
          <li><a href="multi-col-menu.html">Multiple Column Men
          <li class="has-children"> <a href="#" class="current">
            <ul>
              <li><a href="tall-button-header.html">Tall But
              <li><a href="image-logo.html">Image Logo</a></
              <li class="active"><a href="tall-logo.html">Ta
            </ul>
          </li>
          <li class="has-children"> <a href="#">Carousels</a>
            <ul>
              <li><a href="variable-width-slider.html">Variab
                    href="variable-width-slider.html">Testimoni
```

A descriptive URL, also known as a "user-friendly URL" or "clean URL," is a web address that is designed to convey the content or purpose of a web page in a way that's easy to understand. Descriptive URLs typically include keywords or phrases related to the page's content, which makes it easier for other users and search engines to navigate your website.

Regular updates to your website is also good SEO practice. Keep your website up-to-date with fresh content and regular maintenance. An outdated website won't get you any visitors and you'll lose out on sales.

Make sure you implement security features such as SSL certificates to protect user data and build trust. Your web hosting provider should be able to help you with this.

So, how will you know if visitors find your website useful? User testing can help you gather feedback and determine if there are areas where your website needs to be improved.

During user testing, a selected group of participants complete specific scenarios or tasks on the website and they provide feedback about their experiences.

Web developers analyze the results and implement recommended improvements. They can ensure that the site is user-friendly, efficient, and tailored to meet the needs of its audience, which will help you create a more effective online presence for your business.

Creating Content

Creating relevant content for your website is kind of like curating your Instagram feed. It's all about showing your best side and giving your audience what they want to see. It's quite simple really, and you don't have to be able to write like Shakespeare. In fact, you're actually better off if you don't write like a famous literary writer.

Here's how to do it:

- Your website is like your personal online diary. The "About Us" page is your chance to introduce yourself and share your journey. Why did you start your business? What do you love about it? Tell your visitors more about yourself so that they can get to know you.
- Imagine your website as a virtual store. The "Products/Services" page is like your display window. Use fantastic images and videos to showcase what you're offering.
- You should make it easy for people to contact you on your website. Make it easy with a "Contact" page. Provide your email or a contact form so visitors can reach out.
- If you're into blogging, you can have your own space to share your thoughts. It's like a social media feed, but it's all you. Write about what you're passionate about, and your readers will keep coming back.

The trick is to think of your website as your online showcase. Fill it with great content and you'll keep your audience interested and coming back for more!

Hiring External People to Help You Create Your Website

Hiring external professionals to create your website can be a wise decision, especially if you don't have the time or the skills to do it yourself. However, keep in mind that this might take a large chunk of your budget. Set a realistic budget and discuss it with the professionals. Be prepared for additional expenses that may arise during the project.

You'll have to be clear about your needs. Clearly communicate your website's design and the features and functionality you want. The more precise your instructions, the smoother the development process.

It's important that you work actively along with the people who will be designing your website. Make sure you respond to their inquiries and provide them with regular feedback.

Keep the work going by establishing a project timeline with milestones and deadlines.

Also, discuss ongoing maintenance and support. You need to understand who will handle updates, security, and troubleshooting after the website is live. Determine ownership and hosting details and clarify domain ownership.

Regularly review the website during development to provide feedback and ensure it aligns with your vision.

Once the site is live, you also need to check if it aligns with what you initially had in mind for it.

Make sure you know how to maintain the website once it's live, otherwise, you will have to ask the design agency to train you on how to do so.

Hiring professionals to create your website can save you time and lead to a high-quality result while maintaining clear communication.

An E-Commerce Section For Your Website

If you're going to be selling items, you will have to set up an e-commerce section on your website. This will be like opening your own online store.

Imagine your website as a mall, and your e-commerce section is your shop. This is where you can display all your amazing products for the world to see.

Just like Instagram pics, use high-quality images to show your products. Good photos will entice people to buy them.

Think of your website's checkout process as a quick and easy transaction at your favorite snack bar. Ensure it's hassle-free, with secure payment options so customers can pay with confidence.

When someone clicks "Add to Cart," it's like ringing up their order at the cash register. Make sure everything is smooth and efficient, just like when you're checking out at your favorite online stores.

So, setting up your e-commerce section is like having your own online shop—just make sure it's as appealing and user-friendly as your go-to online stores. Your products deserve the spotlight, and your customers deserve a seamless shopping experience.

Registering Your Website With Search Engines

When your website is ready to be launched, you don't just want it hanging out there; you need your potential customers to be able to find it. Registering your site with search engines will put your business on the map in the digital world.

Just like how you'd want your favorite hangout spot to appear on the map app on your phone, you need your website to show up when people search for your business. This is where the search engines like Google, Bing, and Yahoo come into play. You register your website with them. It's almost like adding your business to a directory. This way, when someone types in keywords related to your business, your website will have a better chance of showing up in the search results.

You have to submit a site map when you register your website. Your sitemap is almost like a menu of all the items you offer your customers. On your website, a sitemap is like a list of all the pages and content it contains. By submitting this sitemap to search engines, you're basically telling them to check out all the great stuff on your websites. It makes it easier for search engines to explore and index your site. So when someone's searching for something specific, your site is more likely to pop up in their search results.

How do You Create a Sitemap?

Creating a sitemap for your website is essential for improving its discoverability by search engines. Here's how to create a sitemap.

Manual Sitemap Creation

This method is suitable for smaller websites with a limited number of pages:

- You can create a sitemap manually by listing all the pages on your site.
- Open a text editor or a spreadsheet program like Microsoft Excel or Google Sheets.
- Create a table with two columns: one for the page URL and one for the last modification date.
- List all the pages of your website in the first column, starting with the homepage. You can also add the last modification date for each page.
- Save the file with a name that's easy to recognize, such as "sitemap.xml."

Online Sitemap Generators

For larger websites with many pages, it can take too much time to create a sitemap manually. Online sitemap generators can help you with this process.

- Use a free online sitemap generator like XML-sitemaps.com, Screaming Frog, or Yoast SEO (if you're using WordPress).
- Enter your website's URL.
- You can customize your settings if you want to do so, such as by selecting specific pages.
- Click the "Generate Sitemap" button.
- The tool will create an XML sitemap for your website.
- Download the generated sitemap and save it in your website's root directory.

Content Management Systems (CMS)

If your website is built using a content management system like WordPress you can use plugins to generate and manage your sitemap.

Install and activate an SEO plugin like Yoast SEO or All in One SEO Pack.

When you configure the plugin's sitemap settings it will automatically generate a sitemap for your website.

Once you've created your sitemap you should submit it to major search engines like Google, Bing, and Yahoo using their respective webmaster tools. This will help them index your website's content more efficiently, making it more visible to the different search engines.

Registering Your Website With Google, Bing And Yahoo

Follow these steps to register your website.

Google Search Console

- Go to Google Search Console.
- Sign in with your Google account. If you don't have one, you'll need to create it.
- Click on the "Add URL Prefix" button.
- Enter your website URL and click "Continue."
- Choose a verification method. The easiest way is to use the HTML tag option.
- Copy the provided HTML tag.
- Go to your website's source code and paste the HTML tag within the <head> section.
- Go back to Google Search Console and click "Verify."
- Once verified, you can submit your sitemap to Google.

Bing Webmaster Tools

- Go to Bing Webmaster Tools.
- Sign in with your Microsoft account or create one if you don't have it.
- Click "Add a Site" and enter your website URL.
- Verify ownership by selecting one of the verification methods (e.g., adding a meta tag to your website's home page).
- Once verified you can submit your sitemap to Bing.

Yahoo (via Bing)

Since Yahoo's search results are powered by Bing you don't need to submit your site separately to Yahoo if you've already done so through Bing Webmaster Tools.

Remember to create and submit a sitemap for your website through these tools. A sitemap is like a roadmap for search engines, helping them index your website's pages more effectively.

By registering your website with these major search engines and submitting a sitemap, you'll increase your site's chances of appearing in search results when people look for content related to your business or interests. This is an important step in getting your website noticed on the web.

Testing, Launching, and Maintaining Your Website

Before launching, thoroughly test your website to check for functionality, broken links, and responsive design. Make sure it works well on different web browsers and devices.

You'll also have to implement security measures to protect your website from cyber threats. Regularly update your website's software and plugins. Use SSL certificates to encrypt data transmission and set up strong passwords for site access.

Once everything is in place and you've tested everything, you can launch your website for the world to see. Promote it on your social media accounts and to your network.

Regularly update your website with fresh content, product listings, and information. Make sure you stay informed about website security and SEO best practices.

Monitor your website's performance with analytics tools like Google Analytics. Also, ask your users and customers for feedback which will help you continuously improve your website.

WORKSHEET: TEENAGE ENTREPRENEUR WEBSITE DEVELOPMENT

Completing this worksheet will help you get started on planning your website.

Name:

_____

Business Idea: [Briefly describe your business or project]

_____

Goal: [What do you want to achieve with your website?]

_____

_____

_____

Define Your Website's Purpose

Why are you creating this website? [E.g., To sell my products and services]

_____

_____

_____

Choose a Domain Name

What are your top domain name choices?

_____

_____

_____

Select a Website Building Platform

Which website builder are you considering? [E.g., Site123, Wix, WordPress]

_____

_____

_____

List the features that are important for your website. [E.g., e-commerce capabilities, blogging, gallery]

_____

_____

_____

Website Design

Describe the style and design you envision for your website. [E.g., colorful and playful, minimalist and modern]

_____

_____

_____

What should your website's color scheme be? [E.g., red and white, blue and green]

_____

_____

_____

Do you have a logo? [Yes/No]

_____

_____

_____

Navigation and Layout

Create a sitemap of your website's menu structure. [E.g., Home, About, Products, Contact]

_____

_____

_____

What elements will be on the homepage? [E.g., banner image, introduction]

_____

_____

_____

Mobile Responsiveness

How important is it that your website looks good and functions well on mobile devices? [Very important, somewhat important, not very important]

_____

_____

_____

What elements would have to be optimized for mobile?

_____

_____

_____

Branding

Describe your branding elements (e.g., logo, colors, fonts).

_____

_____

_____

How will you ensure consistency throughout your website?

_____

_____

_____

Content Creation

What content will you create for your website? [E.g., product descriptions, blog posts, customer testimonials]

_____

_____

Who will be responsible for creating content? [You, a friend, a professional]

SEO Strategy

What are some keywords relevant to your business? [E.g., handmade cupcakes, art prints, English tutoring]

How will you incorporate these keywords into your content?

User Testing

Who will be the user testers for your website? [E.g., friends, family, potential customers]

_____

_____

_____

What tasks should they complete during testing? [E.g., buy a product or service, submit a contact form]

_____

_____

_____

How will you gather and analyze feedback from user testing?

_____

_____

_____

Marketing and Promotion

List some ideas for promoting your website and business. [E.g., social media advertising, email marketing, word of mouth]

_____

_____

_____

Security and Data Protection

How will you protect your website and user data? Do you have strong passwords?

_____

_____

_____

Ongoing Maintenance

Who will be responsible for maintaining your website? [You, a web developer]

_____

_____

_____

How often will you update your website's content? Do you have a publishing plan in place?

_____

_____

_____

Feedback and Improvements

How will you gather feedback from website visitors?

_____

_____

_____

What are some possible improvements or additional features you might consider for your website in the future?

_____

_____

_____

Launch Plan

When do you plan to launch your website?

_____

_____

_____

How will you announce the launch to your target audience?

_____

_____

_____

Budget

Create a budget for your website project. Include costs for domain registration, hosting, web development, marketing, and any other expenses.

_____

_____

_____

Next Steps

List the immediate steps you need to take to start building your website.

_____

_____

_____

Deadline

Set a deadline for completing your website development project.

_____

_____

_____

KEY TAKEAWAYS

- A website is a vital tool for any business in the digital age, functioning as a 24/7 digital storefront and a platform for connecting with customers worldwide.
- It's essential for customers to be able to learn about your business, explore your

products/services, and decide whether to buy from you.

- A well-designed and attractive website creates a professional and trustworthy image, setting you apart from competitors.
- Your website serves as an information hub, sharing details about your offerings, contact information, pricing, and FAQs.
- Unlike physical stores, your website is available around the clock, allowing customers to access information and buy your products and services at times that are convenient to them.
- Convenience is important, as customers prefer researching and shopping online. Websites enable product browsing and comparison.
- Websites offer a cost-effective way to market and advertise your business, and you can use digital strategies to reach a broad audience.
- Detailed product or service descriptions, high-quality visuals, and videos enhance customer understanding.
- Websites support content marketing, demonstrating your expertise in your industry through blog posts, articles, and guides.
- As your business expands, your website can grow with it, accommodating more pages, features, and capabilities.
- To create a website, start by defining its purpose, selecting a domain name, choosing a website

builder and hosting provider, and designing a user-friendly and responsive layout.

- Consider user-friendly navigation, mobile responsiveness, brand consistency, fast loading times, high-resolution visuals, readable fonts, effective use of white space, and accessible content.
- Avoid excessive pop-ups and prioritize essential elements. You should also incorporate social media icons and share buttons.
- For better search engine visibility, focus on SEO practices by optimizing meta tags, descriptive URLs, regular content updates, and security measures.
- Sitemaps are essential for search engine indexing; they can be created manually, with online generators, or through content management systems.
- Register your website with search engines like Google, Bing, and Yahoo to help them become more discoverable, and submit your sitemap to help them index your content.
- Before you launch your website, test it for functionality, responsive design, and security. Regularly update and maintain it, and use feedback from users to improve it.

STRATEGY 8

MONEY MASTERY FOR YOUR FIRST BUSINESS

Formal education will make you a living. Self-education will make you a fortune.

— JIM ROHN

Starting your own business as a teen is like leveling up in the game of life. You're already way ahead of your peers if you're an entrepreneur. It's all about taking your cool ideas and turning them into real-life money-makers. You've worked on your marketing strategy, and you have established a social media platform and a website, so the word about your business is officially out there. But there's another secret weapon you need for this epic adventure: financial management.

We're going to show you the key tricks and tips to kick-start your business, manage your money, and become a financial wizard. From creating your money plans to understanding how it flows in and out, setting your prices, and even building a shield for unexpected surprises, we'll guide you on this awesome journey of success in the entrepreneurial world.

KICKSTARTING YOUR FINANCIAL MANAGEMENT JOURNEY

Starting a business as a teenager can be an exciting and educational experience. However, effective financial management is crucial for the success and sustainability of your business, and that can be tricky and scary when you're just starting out. Here are some financial management tips tailored to a teenager starting their first business:

Create a Budget

Begin by creating a comprehensive budget that sets out your expected income and expenses. This will help you understand your financial needs and limitations.

Open a Business Bank Account

Open a separate business bank account. If you have a separate account for your business and personal expenses, it makes it easier to track your business finances and it will be easier to work out the tax that your business needs to pay.

Record Keeping

Maintain organized records of all your financial transactions. This includes invoices, receipts, and statements. Using accounting software or a spreadsheet can also help you with this process.

Set Clear Financial Goals

Establish clear financial goals for your business, including revenue targets, expense limits, and profit margins. Having specific objectives will help you stay focused and become more successful in the long term.

Monitor Cash Flow

Regularly track your cash flow, which is the money coming in and going out of your business. Cash flow management is important to cover your day-to-day expenses.

Cost Control

Be frugal and find ways to minimize expenses. Consider purchasing second-hand equipment or finding cost-effective suppliers. Avoid unnecessary spending such as spending money on transport by holding most of your meetings online. In the past, businesses used to spend a lot of money on transport and food for meetings, and this cost can be avoided when meetings are held virtually.

Pricing Strategy

Carefully set your prices to cover your costs and make sure you can generate a profit. Research your competitors' pricing to ensure your rates are competitive.

Invoicing and Payment Terms

Create clear and professional invoices for your customers. Set reasonable payment terms, and follow up on unpaid invoices promptly.

Savings and Emergency Fund

Set some of the money you make aside for emergency expenses. If your business faces hard times at some stage, you still want to be able to forge ahead.

Taxes

You need to understand how your tax situation will work, and how you can set some money aside to pay your taxes. A tax professional and accounting software can help you deal with this.

Financial Education

Invest time in learning about basic financial concepts, including profit and loss, balance sheets, and cash flow statements. This knowledge will you make informed financial decisions. Take some classes in accounting to learn more.

Seek Advice

Ask mentors for advice, as well as experienced entrepreneurs, or even family members who have financial expertise.

Invest in Learning

Consider taking courses or attending workshops related to financial management for small businesses. There are many courses and other resources available online that can help you.

Track Your Business Performance

Regularly review your financial statements, assess your business's performance, and adjust your strategies as needed.

USEFUL ACCOUNTING SOFTWARE

Maybe you think accounting software sounds boring, but it can save you a lot of time and effort and contribute to your business's success.

You might even wonder if you really need this type of software. Well, imagine this: you're running your own business, selling the products and services you've designed and things are taking off. Money's coming in, but where is it going? How much profit are you really making? That's where accounting software can be your secret weapon. It's like having a financial sidekick that helps you keep track of every dollar and cent so you can focus on doing business.

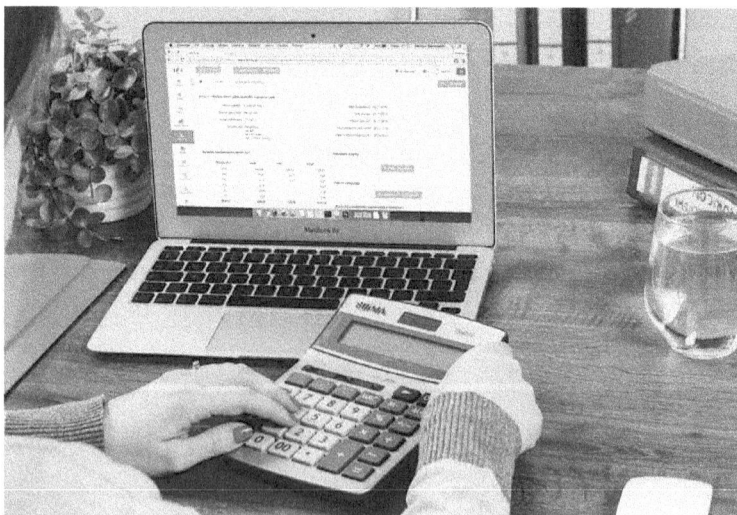

So, how can accounting software help you?

Accounting software isn't some boring number-crunching tool. It can help you figure out your sales, expenses, and profits pretty quickly, and you don't have to spend forever trying to figure out the math by scribbling numbers on paper. You can focus on what's really important to you, while still feeling like a financial wizard.

As a teenpreneur, your days are probably already jam-packed. You're working on your business, studying, and also trying to run a social life. Accounting software saves you time by automating tasks like invoicing and tracking expenses. That means more time for doing the stuff you really enjoy doing.

Want to buy a new gadget or save up for tickets for that awesome concert you want to attend? Accounting software helps you create budgets and stick to them. You can set goals and track your progress without having to worry about complicated ways of doing it.

Most accounting software is super user-friendly and visually appealing. It's designed to be intuitive, making it easy for you to understand your financial picture.

If you have a team or partners in your business, you can invite them to collaborate on the software. It's like working together on a digital project, which is way cooler than spending all your precious time doing boring spreadsheets.

With accounting software, you can plan for the future. It helps you make smart decisions by providing insights into what's working and what's not. It can help you see how to bring your business into the future.

Many accounting software options have mobile apps. You can check your finances on the go, whether you're at a friend's house or waiting for the bus. Your business is in your pocket!

Accounting software can teach you valuable financial skills. You'll learn about cash flow, financial health, and how to manage money like a pro. These skills will serve you well, no matter where life takes you.

You're probably wondering, what is the best type of accounting software for teenage entrepreneurs? There are a number of options available.

When you choose software for your business, you need to consider the following factors:

When choosing accounting software, consider the following factors:

- What specific accounting tasks do you need to perform? Choose software that will make it easier for you to run your business.
- Look for software with an intuitive and user-friendly interface, especially if you're new to accounting. You don't want to waste your

precious time trying to figure out how a program works, and then getting nothing else done.

- Many accounting software options offer free trials or have free versions, making them accessible to teenage entrepreneurs. Consider your budget and choose software that fits your budget.
- If you need to access your financial information while rushing through your busy life, you can choose software with a mobile app.
- Consider whether the software can grow with your business. If you plan to expand, you need to choose software that can accommodate your future needs.
- Check if the software provider offers customer support and educational resources to help you get the most out of the software.

Some of the following options might be suitable for your business:

- QuickBooks has a user-friendly interface and a range of features. It's a great choice for small businesses and startups. It offers a free trial, which means it's accessible to you if you're just looking to get started with this type of software.
- Wave is a free accounting and invoicing software that's perfect for small businesses and freelancers. It offers a user-friendly interface and features like

income and expense tracking, invoicing, and financial reports.

- Zoho Books is an affordable, cloud-based accounting software that offers invoicing, expense tracking, and basic accounting features.
- FreshBooks is user-friendly and designed for self-employed people and small business owners. It offers features like invoicing, expense tracking, and time tracking.
- Xero is a more advanced accounting software suitable for small to medium-sized businesses. It offers a wide range of features, including multi-currency support, inventory management, and the ability to handle multiple businesses.

A Story About Teen Financial Wizards

A group of high school friends decided to start a business together. Max, Emma, Olivia, and Liam shared a passion for creating custom-designed phone cases and T-shirts. It started as their hobby, but they managed to turn it into a successful business.

As their business grew, so did their ambition to manage their finances more efficiently. They knew they needed a tool that could help them understand the money side of things. Then Emma had an idea that would change their entrepreneurial journey forever.

She told the others that they needed accounting software to help them keep track of their money, as it would make their lives much easier and give them the time to focus on what's really important.

The others agreed, and they decided to embark on this financial adventure together. They spent days researching different accounting software options and ultimately found one they liked and that was easy to use.

With their newfound tool, the Teenpreneurs began to understand their business's financial health better than ever before. Max, the creative genius, continued to design and print their products. Olivia, the tech-savvy member of the team, took charge of setting up the software and connecting it to their bank accounts. Liam tracked and categorized their expenses. Emma, the communicator, managed customer invoices and payments. Everyone had a role to play.

As they delved into their financial records, they gained a better understanding of their profits, costs, and sales patterns. The colorful charts and graphs helped them visualize their financial progress, and the entire process became even more exciting to them.

One day, Olivia discovered that their line of phone covers was their most profitable product. Armed with this knowledge, they decided to invest more time and resources in that area. They also noticed that spending on promotional materials wasn't getting them the results they desired so they reevaluated their marketing strategies.

Their accounting software became their financial compass, helping them set and achieve their goals. They established a budget for their next product launch and tracked their spending closely. The software alerted them when their expenses exceeded the budget, acting like a responsible guardian of their treasure.

The friends' business flourished. With their strong financial knowledge and the insights gained from their accounting software, they expanded their product line and even attracted international customers. They were savvy business owners who managed to turn their hobby into a successful business.

BUDGETING FOR YOUR STARTUP—A STEP-BY-STEP GUIDE

Budgeting is one of the most important things you can do when starting your new business. You can use this step-by-step guide to make things easier for yourself.

Look at Your Finances

Look at how much money you have available to spend on your business. This will include money you get from your parents and possibly other people who want to invest in your business. Perhaps you have held part-time jobs such as delivering newspapers, or you've worked as a waitress.

If you've managed to save some of this money, you can also use this for your business.

Set Clear Goals

Define your short-term and long-term financial goals. This could include startup costs, the monthly costs of operating your business, and how much profit you want to make.

Create a Business Budget

Separate your business and personal finances. Develop a detailed budget for your business that covers all expenses, including:

- Your costs for starting the business. This would be one-time expenses like equipment, licenses, and initial marketing.
- The money you will spend to keep your business operating. This will include ongoing costs such as rent, utilities, salaries, and materials.
- Estimate how much your income will be, based on sales, pricing, and market research.

Emergency Fund

You should also build an emergency fund that can help your business during tough times. This savings buffer can help you cover unexpected business or personal expenses. For example, if you run a business that bakes healthy snacks, and the cost of your ingredients suddenly goes up due to an increase in inflation.

Track Expenses

Make sure you keep track of how much money your business spends, as this will directly influence your profit. The accounting software that we discussed can also help you with this.

Monitor Cash Flow

You also need to keep track of how much money you spend in your business, as you could potentially suffer losses if you spend too much money.

Prioritize Expenses

Identify your essential business and personal expenses. Once you've prioritized expenses, you'll also be better able to see where you can do cost-cutting, when you need to do so.

Save for Taxes

It's important to set some money aside for taxes. Consult with a tax professional to understand your tax obligations and ensure compliance.

Invest Wisely

When you make money, make sure you invest it wisely. Invest at least some of it back into your business.

Review and Amend Your Budget

Regularly review your budget to track your progress, make adjustments, and ensure you're on track to meet your financial goals.

Maintain Discipline

Stick to your budget and avoid unnecessary expenses and impulse spending that could cause you financial trouble in the long run.

HOW CAN YOU GET EXTERNAL FINANCING FOR YOUR BUSINESS?

If you prepare well, and you have business strategies in place, you should be able to get funding for your business like any other adult entrepreneur.

Here's how you can explore external funding options.

It is often best to start out by seeking support from family and friends who believe in your business idea. Be clear about the terms, repayment plans, and potential risks to maintain healthy relationships. You don't want to burn your bridges and find yourself in a situation where people don't trust you anymore because you owe them money.

Grants

Another option is to look for business grants and competitions specifically designed for young entrepreneurs.

Organizations, schools, and government agencies often offer such opportunities. These grants can be a source of non-repayable funding.

Angel Investors

Then you get the wonderful people called angel investors.

Angel investors are rich people who invest in startup businesses in exchange for ownership equity or convertible debt. They are typically early-stage investors, providing vital financial support and often offering valuable mentorship and industry expertise.

Many of them are prepared to take risks, and they're willing to invest in high-potential startups. Their investment amounts can vary widely, and they often expect a return on their investment through an exit strategy, such as a merger, acquisition, or initial public offering in the future. Angel investors can operate individually or join investment groups, and their contributions can be a significant source of capital for entrepreneurs.

Some angel investors are open to investing in teen-owned businesses, especially if they see potential in your idea. Be prepared to pitch your business confidently and professionally.

Crowdfunding

Platforms like Kickstarter and Indiegogo allow you to raise funds from a crowd of supporters who believe in your project. Crowdfunding can be an effective way to fund product development or a specific project.

Mentorship and Networking

Connect with experienced entrepreneurs, mentors, and local business organizations. They can provide guidance, connections, and, in some cases, financial support.

Business Incubators and Accelerators

Some incubators and accelerators, such as the Young Entrepreneur Council (YEC) programs, cater to teen entrepreneurs. These programs often provide funding, mentorship, and resources in exchange for equity or a fee.

Microloans

Look at microloan programs tailored for young entrepreneurs. These loans, often provided by nonprofit organizations, can be used for various business needs.

Online Lenders

Consider online lending platforms that may have more flexible requirements than traditional banks. Some of these lenders are open to working with younger business owners.

Competitions and Scholarships

Search for entrepreneurship competitions and scholarships that offer financial prizes to young entrepreneurs.

These can provide both funding and recognition for your business.

Educational Institutions

Some schools or universities have entrepreneurship programs that offer funding, resources, and support to student entrepreneurs. Check if your school or college doesn't have such opportunities.

Local Business Grants

Investigate local or regional grants and funding programs aimed at supporting small businesses. Your location may offer opportunities for funding.

Small Business Associations

National or regional small business associations may have programs or grants designed to support young entrepreneurs. Check with organizations like the Small Business Administration (SBA).

When you're looking for external funding, you need to do the following:

- Develop a strong and professional business plan.
- Be clear and explain how you will use the funds and the potential return on investment.
- Ask experienced entrepreneurs what you can do to improve your pitch and strategy.

- Demonstrate your passion and commitment to your business idea.
- Interact in a professional way with potential investors or funders.
- If you're well prepared and confident when you do your proposition, it will increase your chances of obtaining the funding you need to launch and grow your business.

WORKSHEET: BUSINESS FUNDING PROPOSAL

Here's a worksheet that outlines the key elements to include in your funding proposal. You can base your proposal on the template below.

Cover Page

Title: Your Business Name

Your Name

Contact Information (Address, Phone, Email)

Date

Executive Summary

Provide a brief overview of your business idea.

Describe the amount of funding you are seeking and how you plan to use it.

Highlight what makes your business unique and its growth potential.

Business Description

Provide a detailed description of your business, including its mission, vision, and goals.

Explain your target market and your products or services.

Share your business's legal structure (e.g., sole proprietorship, LLC) and location.

Market Research

Summarize your market research findings, including market size, trends, and competition.

Demonstrate a clear understanding of your target market and its needs.

Financial Projections

Present your financial projections, including income statements, cash flow statements, and balance sheets for at least the next two years.

Describe and show how the funding will impact your business's financials and profitability.

Use of Funds

Detail your plan to use the requested funding. Include a breakdown of expenses, such as marketing, product development, equipment, or hiring.

Business Plan

Provide an overview of your business plan, including strategies for growth and business expansion.

Explain how the funding will help you achieve your business goals.

Marketing and Sales Strategy

Describe your marketing and sales strategies to get and keep customers.

Highlight any innovative approaches or advantages you have in the market.

Management Team

Introduce your management team, including their backgrounds and roles.

Emphasize any unique skills, experience, or expertise that sets your team apart. If you're the only person working in the business, describe your skills and experience.

Competitive Analysis

Analyze your competitors and explain your competitive advantage.

Address how you plan to maintain or strengthen your position in the market.

Exit Strategy

Provide a timeline for when investors can expect returns on their investment.

Risks and Mitigation

Identify potential risks and challenges your business may face.

Explain how you plan to mitigate these risks and uncertainties.

Request for Funding

Specify the exact amount of funding you need from investors.

Provide details about the type of funding (e.g., equity investment, convertible note, loan) you are open to.

Appendix

Include any supporting documents, such as resumes, market research data, product images, or testimonials.

You can adapt this worksheet to suit your business and its unique characteristics. A well-prepared funding proposal is essential to convince potential investors of the viability of your business.

KEY TAKEAWAYS

- Financial management is a crucial aspect of starting a business.
- Key financial management tips for teenage entrepreneurs include creating a budget, opening a separate business bank account, maintaining organized records, setting clear financial goals, monitoring cash flow, controlling costs, setting pricing strategies, managing invoicing and payment terms, saving for emergencies, understanding taxes, investing in financial education, seeking advice from mentors and experts, and tracking business performance.
- Accounting software can be a valuable tool for teenage entrepreneurs, helping them manage their finances efficiently and make informed decisions. It automates tasks, saves time, helps with

budgeting, offers user-friendly interfaces, and provides insights for future planning.

- When choosing accounting software, consider factors such as your specific accounting needs, user-friendliness, cost, mobile accessibility, scalability, customer support, and educational resources.

- Teen entrepreneurs can explore external funding options for their businesses, including seeking support from family and friends, applying for grants and scholarships, attracting angel investors, using crowdfunding platforms, building mentorship and networking relationships, participating in business incubators and accelerators, accessing microloans, working with online lenders, and participating in business competitions.

- To secure external funding, teenage entrepreneurs should prepare a professional business plan, clearly explain how the funds will be used, demonstrate passion and commitment, and interact professionally with potential investors or funders.

- A well-prepared funding proposal is essential for convincing potential investors of the viability and potential of your business.

CONCLUSION

In the closing chapter of this book, we empower you, teens, to balance entrepreneurship and a healthy lifestyle. We offer you practical strategies, resources, and motivation to help you get started on your journey to becoming successful and healthy entrepreneurs.

We've looked at the following strategies:

- **Goal Setting:** The importance of setting clear and achievable goals for both their business and personal well-being.
- **Time Management:** Helping you manage your time effectively will ensure that you can balance your entrepreneurial endeavors with self-care.
- **Financial Literacy:** Educating you on the fundamentals of financial management and wealth-building.

- **Mental Health:** Highlighting the significance of mental health and providing you with tips on how to maintain a healthy mindset while pursuing entrepreneurship.
- **Networking:** We encourage you to build a strong network to support your entrepreneurial aspirations.

Resources For Your Further Learning And Development:

- **Nomads with a Purpose:** Offers guidance on teaching entrepreneurship to teens. (https://www. nomadswithapurpose.com/teaching-entrepreneurship-to-teens/)
- **Career Addict:** Provides insights and advice for teen entrepreneurs. (https://www.careeraddict. com/teen-entrepreneurs)
- **PlanStreet Inc:** Explains the importance of mental health and well-being. (https://www. planstreetinc.com/top-ten-reasons-why-mental-health-is-so-important/)

While becoming a healthypreneur may seem daunting, it's entirely doable if you take it one step at a time. The key is to balance entrepreneurship with a healthy lifestyle, and the book offers you tools to achieve this.

Finally, the key takeaway is that you can achieve both entrepreneurial success and a healthy lifestyle by setting clear goals, managing time effectively, mastering financial literacy, prioritizing mental health, and building a strong network of support.

So, don't wait any longer to start building wealth and become an entrepreneur, all while maintaining your health. Take action now, as outlined in this book.

As we close this chapter and set forth on your healthypreneurial journey, remember this: "You, as a teenage healthypreneur, are on the cusp of something extraordinary. The world is yours to shape, not just in terms of wealth, but in terms of well-being, wisdom, and impact. The journey is yours to chart, and I have no doubt that it will be nothing short of remarkable."

If you've found this book to be a helpful companion, I invite you to share your thoughts with a review. Your feedback can serve as a guiding light for other teens embarking on a similar path to success and well-being. And while you're exploring, remember to check out my other books, "The Teenage Wealthypreneur" and "Ink of Tears: Echoes of Shattered Souls Poetry Collections," where you'll find additional inspiration and guidance for your remarkable journey in life!

REFERENCES

Alaska Business. (2019, November 7) *Research Shows 41 Percent of Teens Would Consider Starting Business as Career Option.*. Alaska Business Magazine. https://www.akbizmag.com/monitor/national-entrepre neurship-month-research-shows-41-percent-of-teens-would-consider-starting-business-as-career-option/

Barrett, B. (2023, January 30). *Lessons from a young entrepreneur | Ep 422.* ChooseFI. https://www.choosefi.com/lessons-from-a-young-entrepreneur-ep-422/

Baskin, K. (2019, December 31). *The 7 superpowers of resilience.* MeQuilibrium. https://www.mequilibrium.com/resources/the-7-superpowers-of-resilience/

Career Addict. (2018, November 14). *The 9 Most Successful Teen Entrepreneurs in the World.* CareerAddict. https://www.careeraddict. com/teen-entrepreneurs

Daniel, Farrah, & Hardy, Adam. (2021, April 13). *How to make a website for your brand or small business.* Forbes. https://www.forbes.com/advisor/business/how-to-make-a-website-for-your-business/

Gabi. (2022, May 21). *Teaching entrepreneurship to teens [Ultimate How-to Guide].* Nomads with a Purpose. https://www.nomadswithapur pose.com/teaching-entrepreneurship-to-teens/

Gordon-Barnes, C. (2014, October 12). *6 fresh ways to find your passion.* Themuse.com; The Muse. https://www.themuse.com/advice/6-fresh-ways-to-find-your-passion

Greenberg, M. (n.d.). 8 Ways to Bounce Back After a Disappointment | Psychology Today. Www.psychologytoday.com. https://www.psychol ogytoday.com/us/blog/the-mindful-self-express/201506/8-ways-bounce-back-after-disappointment

Hussain, A. (2018). *7 habits of highly effective people [Book Summary].* Hubspot.com. https://blog.hubspot.com/sales/habits-of-highly-effective-people-summary

Lodge, M. (2019, October 25). *10 successful young entrepreneurs.*

Investopedia. https://www.investopedia.com/10-successful-young-entrepreneurs-4773310

Macready, H. (2022, November 7). *How to use social media for small business: 11 simple tips.* Hootsuite Social Media Management. https://blog.hootsuite.com/social-media-tips-for-small-business-owners/

Page, M. (n.d.). *5 tips to better your time management | Michael Page US.* Michael Page. https://www.michaelpage.com/advice/career-advice/growing-your-career/5-tips-better-your-time-management

Panel, E. (n.d.). *Council post: 10 ways to live a healthier lifestyle as an entrepreneur.* Forbes. Retrieved October 27, 2023, from https://www.forbes.com/sites/theyec/2021/08/12/10-ways-to-live-a-healthier-lifestyle-as-an-entrepreneur/?sh=3e83c1046de6

Parker, T. (2020, June 17). *The basics of financing a business.* Investopedia. https://www.investopedia.com/articles/pf/13/business-financing-primer.asp

Rebic, D. (2022, August 15). *5 lessons we learned from the body keeps the score.* Myndlift. https://www.myndlift.com/post/5-lessons-we-learned-from-the-body-keeps-the-score

Shopify Staff. *What is entrepreneurship? Definition and guide for 2022.* (n.d.). Shopify. https://www.shopify.com/ca/blog/what-is-entrepreneurship

Stowers, J. (2019). *A step by step guide to starting a business.* Business News Daily. https://www.businessnewsdaily.com/4686-how-to-start-a-business.html

www.ingramcontent.com/pod-product-compliance
Lightning Source LLC
Chambersburg PA
CBHW052017030426

42335CB00026B/3177